D0849146

PUTTING CHILDREN'S INTERESTS FIRST IN U.S. FAMILY LAW AND POLICY

The well-being of children should be a social priority, and should consider the family circumstances into which children are born. *Putting Children's Interests First in US Family Law and Policy: With Power Comes Responsibility* details the rise of a federal policy of "sexual expressionism", which prioritizes adults' interests over children's welfare. It describes the costs to children in the areas of family structure and stability, and the federal programs attempting to ameliorate the situation of non-marital children. Offering a detailed empirical and ethical critique both of "sexual expressionism" and of the related federal programs, this study will be of interest to scholars and activists supporting children, women and the poor.

Helen M. Alvaré is Professor of Law at the Scalia Law School at George Mason University, Virginia, where she teaches family law. For over three decades she has practiced or taught family law and constitutional law, and writes in both scholarly and popular venues about the welfare of women and children. She has been an ABC news consultant, a *Time Magazine* "40 Under 40," an advisor to the National Institute on Child Health and Human Development, and a delegate to United Nations' meetings on women. She received her J.D. from Cornell University.

Putting Children's Interests First in U.S. Family Law and Policy

WITH POWER COMES RESPONSIBILITY

HELEN M. ALVARÉ

Scalia Law School
George Mason University

CAMBRIDGE
UNIVERSITY PRESS

CAMBRIDGE
UNIVERSITY PRESS

University Printing House, Cambridge CB2 8BS, United Kingdom

One Liberty Plaza, 20th Floor, New York, NY 10006, USA

477 Williamstown Road, Port Melbourne, VIC 3207, Australia

4843/24, 2nd Floor, Ansari Road, Daryaganj, Delhi – 110002, India

79 Anson Road, #06-04/06, Singapore 079906

Cambridge University Press is part of the University of Cambridge.

It furthers the University's mission by disseminating knowledge in the pursuit of education, learning, and research at the highest international levels of excellence.

www.cambridge.org
Information on this title: www.cambridge.org/9781107176492
DOI: 10.1017/9781316817025

© Helen M. Alvaré 2018

First published 2018

Printed in the United States of America by Sheridan Books, Inc

A catalogue record for this publication is available from the British Library.

ISBN 978-1-107-17649-2 Hardback

To my husband Brian
Who makes seemingly impossible things possible

Contents

Acknowledgments

This was a difficult book to write, not least because it goes against the grain of so much that is "accepted wisdom" in family law and policy. I could not have written it without the strong support of an academic institution which consistently encourages the free play of ideas. When I began to teach at the Scalia Law School at George Mason University, one of my colleagues asked me if I "had come to play." Was I willing to take difficult positions if that was where my research led me? The atmosphere at Scalia Law School makes it infinitely easier to answer affirmatively. I thank Deans Polsby and Butler and my colleagues of these last eight years, for their consistent, thoughtful and challenging support. I am also grateful for the summer research grants which have allowed me to focus on this project in a concentrated manner.

Nearly twenty years ago, law professor William Wagner asked me the question which started the wheels turning that led to this book. I remain grateful for the interest he took in a rookie scholar.

I could never have written this book without the unflagging and talented research assistance of Brian Miller, and Scalia Law librarians Melanie Knapp and Esther Koblenz. I am further grateful for my colleague Meg McDonnell, for sorting through all these ideas with me over the last five years. I am utterly at a loss as to how I have retained the friendship and goodwill of these fine people after having asked for so much, so fast.

My husband Brian and my children Catherine, Julian and Robert Paul, bore with my long mental and physical absences from the house with tremendous good will. They listened to my ideas with an invaluable "ear" for both common sense and compassion to others. Thank you.

Introduction

Nearly twenty years ago a colleague asked me a question I couldn't fully answer. He asked whether, since the 1960s – when the Supreme Court had begun, rightly, to strike down state laws disadvantaging "illegitimate" children – US family law possessed other tools which would encourage men and women to avoid nonmarital childbearing, and instead give their children the advantage of a marital home.

The short answer is no. There are no legal "sticks" available to encourage childbearing within marriage, though there remain emotional and cultural "carrots." In the United States, although a minority of states retain laws punishing adultery, cohabitation, or fornication, and some states continue to resist calls to abolish these, such laws are regularly unenforced.[1] Furthermore, laws penalizing welfare recipients for having a "man in the house" or an illegitimate birth, disappeared in the 1960s.

Mature reflection on the last fifty years, however, yields a surprising discovery. Over this same time period, federal law- and policy-makers have moved in the opposite direction, opting to stress adults' individual rights over children's wellbeing. In particular, they have chosen to valorize the adult sexual behavior which can give rise to nonmarital births, and undermine the stable partnership children need. Especially in judicial opinions, executive agency regulations and publications, federal actors emphasize the importance of individual adults' sexual expression, and its close association with profound human goods, such as dignity, freedom, equality and identity. They are simultaneously silent about, or indifferent to, the sexual partners' marital status, and to the fact that children's family structure is regularly determined at the time of their conception.

---

[1] See Joanne Sweeny, "Undead Statutes: The Rise, Fall and Continuing Uses of Adultery and Fornication Criminal Laws," *University of Chicago Law Journal* 46 (2014): 127–173.

Yet it is well accepted in the sociological, economic, neurological and psychological literature that children's family structure can play a causal role in their long-term welfare, alongside other factors. On average, children born nonmaritally will experience worse economic, educational and emotional outcomes than the children of a married couple, even controlling for their parents' income and education. Unmarried women who give birth to a child experience more relationship transitions: their children are more likely to experience household instability, whether or not their mother is cohabiting with their father at birth.

Throughout the book, I refer to the federal stance as "sexual expressionism:" valorizing adult sexual expression, while remaining silent or indifferent regarding the adult's marital status, and to the reality that children's family structure is usually established at conception. It is most visible in federal speech concerning adults, not teens, although it is adults (over twenty) who give rise to eighty-six percent of nonmarital births.[2] I discuss federal law and policy only, both for reasons of length, and because the federal view is so starkly individualistic and so surprising. The US Supreme Court employs the most emphatic sexual expressionist language, but the executive branch has not lagged far behind.

In their defense, federal actors were inclined to believe that they could have their cake and eat it too, due nearly entirely to the invention and widespread adoption of hormonal birth control following the 1960s. The government believed that it could denounce sexual repression and facilitate sex without children, while simultaneously ending inequality between men and women and ensuring that every child was "intended." Poverty, as we knew it, could be ended. The logic seemed compelling, and even compassionate.

On balance, however, history has not been kind to these expectations. Certainly, the last fifty to sixty years have yielded some positive developments where sexual expression, women and the family are concerned. We have witnessed the acceptance of sexual functioning as a normal and healthy part of both sexes' human existence and happiness. Women's essential human equality is far better acknowledged. Women are taking full advantage of the opportunities opened up to them in the public and private sectors. There is a far greater willingness within the private sphere of marriage, too, to avoid externally imposed role limitations upon women.

---

[2] US Centers for Disease Control, *National Vital Statistics Reports: Births: Final Data for 2014*, by Brady E. Hamilton et al., National Center for Health Statistics (Hyattsville, MD, 2015), www.cdc.gov/nchs/data/nvsr/nvsr64/nvsr64_12.pdf.

At the same time, however, and contrary to original expectations, rates of "unintended" and nonmarital births increased[3] rather than decreased, even after the introduction of expansive federal birth control programs. New patterns of nonmarital sexual activity did not promote couple stability, nor a coherent freedom for women. Divorce rates are high. Cohabitation rates have soared, but the unions are unstable, subject to couples' conflicting interpretations and decreasingly likely to lead to marriage. Women today lead over eighty percent of single-parent households. Women are also increasingly dissatisfied with the markets for sex and marriage shaped by the unlinking of sex from marriage, and even from the idea of children. A major study of women's subjective wellbeing, in 2009, reported that women were less happy than they had been thirty-five years previously, and less happy than men.[4] It is only natural to wonder if dramatic changes in our sex, marriage and parenting environments played a role.

Regarding expectations for contraception, even the experts at governmental agencies and their partners overseeing contraception programs are frustrated by the failure rates and side effects of existing methods. They find themselves seeking entirely new methods, and promoting the substitution of longer-acting forms – "long acting reversible contraceptives" or "LARCs"–although these remain unpopular with women, and burdened with ethical and safety questions.

At the same time, economic forces, labor markets and technological developments have combined to weaken job prospects for men and women with fewer years of education. Men have been hit particularly hard. For poorer women who live in communities which have fewer working men (and often more men with criminal and drug histories), while they wish to be mothers, marriage and marital parenting seem out of reach. The opportunity costs of being a single parent are not a sufficient deterrent: poorer women have a more difficult time achieving college, marriage or a good job. Furthermore, nonmarital parenting has a tendency to persist down the generations. Due to this and other factors, more than a few researchers link family structure effects with increasing and disturbing economic and achievement gaps between rich and poor, white and black, and even female and male.

---

[3] US Centers for Disease Control, *Recent Declines in Nonmarital Childbearing in the United States*, by Sally C. Curtin et al., National Center for Health Statistics (Hyattsvylle, MD, 2014), www.cdc.gov/nchs/data/databriefs/db162.pdf.; see also the material on nonmarital births in Chapter Two.

[4] Betsey Stevenson and Justin Wolfers, "The Paradox of Declining Female Happiness" (NBER Working Paper No. 14969, May 2009).

Even in the face of all of this, and given the need for fresh ideas, it remains dangerous to write about nonmarital births. The ghost of "illegitimacy" law – which punished nonmarital children as a means of affecting adult behavior – haunts such a project. There is a fear of reviving stigma for single mothers and their children. Consider the cautionary tale of Daniel Patrick Moynihan, whose 1965 study[5] of nonmarital births among black Americans launched a thousand reprisals based on claims that it was racist, anti-poor and anti-family-diversity. Defenders of marital parenting today also face claims that marriage is intrinsically sexist or even violent.

Proposals to reduce nonmarital births also run into conflict with claims of citizens' privacy in their domestic and sexual lives, as well as powerful objections framed in terms of anti-essentialism, or the folly and pride of a universalizing project. Finally, one is always subject to the conversation-stopping objection that a project is "nostalgic" or designed to "turn back the clock."

In spite of all of these substantial and discouraging headwinds, I propose that it is an auspicious time to launch a serious conversation about nonmarital births, and about parental and governmental responsibilities respecting them. Emerging science on the subject continues to illuminate. Thanks to careful and exhaustive scholarship, we understand better today the pathways connecting nonmarital parenting and child outcomes. We also have at our disposal fifty years of national experimentation both with birth control programs and with programs designed to help disadvantaged children "catch-up." The results are not only unsatisfying but sometimes alarming. Many governmental programs for the less-advantaged produce only modest results or worse. And disturbing racial and socioeconomic divisions linked to family structure are emerging. It also does not appear that an economy retooled to provide poor and blue-collar communities with steady employment is around the corner. Something new is needed to assist children, who are all of us. One missing and previously underexplored possibility is the subject of this book: reversing government-endorsed sexual expressionism, and acting rather to encourage and capacitate adults' responsibility to children, beginning at conception when a child's family structure begins.

Today, proposals to strengthen relationships between men and women, and to promote marital childbearing, are less likely to elicit fears that their underlying goals are sexist, racist, anti-LGBT, or directed toward eliminating birth control. The human rights of women, racial minorities and LGBT citizens are on a far more secure footing than during previous decades. Birth

---

5   US Department of Labor, *The Negro Family: The Case for National Action*, by Daniel Patrick Moynihan, U.S. Department of Labor (Washington, D.C., 1965).

control is ubiquitous and in no danger of being sidelined by any political party now in existence in the United States. Men and women of every racial and socioeconomic background still prize marriage and marital parenting. Experts and elected officials across the political spectrum generally agree that marital childbearing is a personal and social good, and that its decline harms poorer Americans in particular. The link between nonmarital birth and widening social gaps – gaps between higher and lower socioeconomic groups, and between the races – troubles Americans' ideals of freedom, equality and social mobility for all.

In light of these new baselines and our far better knowledge about the stakes for children, efforts to curb nonmarital parenting can be understood precisely as forward thinking, not nostalgic. In fact, it is our improved national commitment to equality between races, sexes and socioeconomic groups which makes these efforts necessary, and which can set them on a new foundation. To do nothing seems the equivalent of expecting nothing, and hoping for nothing, for the most disadvantaged families and their children.

Perhaps this book is also timely in light of the national soul-searching which followed the presidential election of 2016. Even the most advantaged Americans, who direct our most influential institutions – politics, the media, the academy and the entertainment industry – acknowledge that they were taken aback at the feelings of class-based powerlessness and rejection reported by many Americans who voted for Donald Trump. With the 2016 election, questions about the possibilities of social mobility, economic security and family stability strode purposefully back into the national spotlight. Scholars and political figures on both sides of the aisle appear motivated to engage them. Children's family structure is a salient element of this conversation. In short, despite the headwinds, this is a good time to have a difficult conversation.

I approach the topic on very narrow grounds: a criticism of the federal government's sexual expressionist stance. This stance ranges from inadequate to recklessly indifferent with respect to nonmarital parenting. It so openly contradicts the emerging scholarly consensus about children's welfare that it is an obvious place to begin. Sexual expressionism can also reduce adults' capacity to form stable partnerships, which adults, children and their communities need. Thus far, the federal government's responses – social welfare and contraception programs – have been insufficient or misconceived, despite the good intentions which animate both.

Regarding the government's social welfare programs, my book is additive. I hope to add a larger concern for children and for marital parenting – especially on behalf of the poor – to the current social welfare agenda. My critique of contraception programs, however, is unlikely to be anticipated or welcome to most observers, many of whom may regard contraception as perhaps the only potentially effective answer, as well as a feminist touchstone. This reaction, however, seems increasingly dated. The pill is nearing its sixtieth anniversary, yet rates of nonmarital birth are at an all-time high. The voice of women is growing. They feel empowered precisely *by* feminism to critique the drugs and devices which alter, not only their bodies, but also the "markets" for sex, dating and marriage – markets which are now shaped in important ways by the separation of sex from children and marriage made possible by contraception.

This book will not address the situation of children reared in single-parent households following a divorce or the death of a parent. It will not consider stepfamilies or adoption or assisted reproductive technologies. It is instead concerned with documenting the government's emphasis on the good of individual adult sexual expression, without paying sufficient attention to the partners' marital status, or to the difficulties faced by the children of unmarried couples.

Chapter One chronicles the federal materials adopting and promoting sexual expressionism. It also considers the interplay between influential cultural and philosophical ideas, and the laws and policies embodying sexual expressionism.

Chapter Two briefly summarizes the social science literature on children's wellbeing as influenced by their nonmarital birth and its common correlates. It also reports on the literature which explains how nonmarital births are fueling extensive economic and social gaps between various groups in the United States. It is the shortest chapter in the book, not because it is unimportant, but on the contrary because it represents decades of exceptional work by dedicated empirical researchers, and grounds an ethical concern for nonmarital children. But I am not a sociologist, and therefore Chapter Two merely reports the work of others in sufficient detail to convey why the government has an ethical responsibility to promote marital, as distinguished from nonmarital, childbearing.

Chapter Three describes the two major types of federal response to nonmarital births: contraception and social welfare programs assisting disadvantaged Americans, including many nonmarital families. It describes the contents of social welfare programs, their costs, and, where available, some of their outcomes. Regarding contraception, it briefly summarizes the history of federal support for contraception programs, and pays special attention to how the government's goals for these programs have shifted over time.

Chapter Four considers both the ethical and anthropological shortcomings of sexual expressionism itself and of the two federal responses. Primarily, it attends to theories about justice for children, but it also considers the immiseration of women and the poor as a result of sexual expressionism.

Chapter Five offers my proposals to reform and reverse sexual expressionism at the federal level, in order to promote governmental and parental responsibility for children's family structure at the moment when family structure usually begins – at conception.

Throughout, I understand that both my analysis and my proposals are a very small piece of the larger puzzle of assisting nonmarital children and their families. The causes and consequences of nonmarital childbearing are many and complex. To date, however, the federal government has regularly put its thumb on the wrong side of the scale: adults' sexual expression.

There is a contemporary tendency to think that this is the only realistic stance in light of current and accepted social mores. I hope this is wrong, and not only because it is an example of the "fallacy of the present" – the tendency to believe that present conditions are inevitable and unchangeable. I also hope it is wrong because people do care about children, who are not only vulnerable, but are all of us. And because the goods of stable family life should be available to everyone in a country which prides itself on fairness, diversity, and opportunity for all – not only for the well off.

1

The Rise of Sexual Expressionism

The leading analysis of sexual practices in the United States, *The Social Organization of Sexuality: Sexual Practices in the United States*, refers to sex as "any mutually voluntary activity with another person that involves genital contact and sexual excitement or arousal."[1] When I speak of sexual expression-*ism*, I am not referring to the endorsing of any particular sexual act, but rather to the valorizing of adults' sexual behavior, including procreative sex, while remaining largely indifferent to the partners' marital status, and to the reality that children's family structure is regularly determined at their conception. To "valorize" sexual expression is to credit it with achieving profound and individualized human goods, such as dignity, freedom, equality and identity.

This chapter contends that federal law and policy demonstrate a sexual expressionist stance, which intersects with various cultural and philosophical trends in ways that strengthen its influence. Several elements within my definition of sexual expressionism will immediately raise questions that require clarification. Allow me to address the five most likely.

First, I am not charging the federal government with failing to think or act in favor of children's overall welfare. Federal programs for born and even unborn children are numerous and well-funded. The Urban Institute estimates that, in 2015, federal expenditure on children totaled 471 billion dollars, with seventy-seven percent representing outlays of federal money, and twenty-three percent representing mostly tax breaks related to the care of children.[2] My claim is rather that the federal government regularly highlights the importance of adults' sexual expression, while remaining indifferent to marriage,

[1] Edward O. Laumann et al., *The Social Organization of Sexuality* (Chicago: University of Chicago Press, 2000), 67.
[2] The Urban Institute, *Kids' Share 2016: Federal Expenditures on Children Through 2015 and Future Projections*, by Sara Edelstein (Washington DC: The Urban Institute, 2016).

and without sufficient or contemporaneous concern for the wellbeing of the children who may be conceived. This is important, in part because children's family structure is so often established at conception, and because family structure can play an important role in child welfare. Using a metaphor suggested by University of Chicago marriage scholar Don Browning, the federal government puts adults' wishes at the "front door" of family formation – at the moment of sexual intercourse.[3] By analogy, when the government creates programs or benefits to assist nonmarital children *after* their conception or birth, it is attending to them at the "back door."

"Back door" programs and benefits are essential as a matter of justice to the vulnerable and as a matter of a nation's attention to the common good. Yet they leave adults' to pursue their plans first and attend to children's needs second. Furthermore, while they certainly merit continued experimentation and refinement, several of the most expensive and most cherished social programs have produced small or inconsistent results, or apply too late in a child's life to make more than a modest difference. It is not even clear that much higher levels of expenditure could close the various gaps between marital and nonmarital children; although it is also likely true that neither major political party in the United States will give it a try in our lifetimes. More and more it appears that even a vast web of interventions will struggle to replace the visible and invisible influences that married parenting can exert upon a child.

Second, it is likely that a majority of Americans, as well as a majority of politicians and family scholars, believe that the federal government's extensive contraception initiatives evidence tremendous concern for children and for channeling births into marriage. For several reasons, however, this is this is not what it appears, nor how matters unfold on the ground.

When a federal voice – that is, members of the federal government or one of its cooperating partners or grantees – addresses contraception, it nearly always speaks first about "preventing unintended pregnancies" and not about "safeguarding children." For example, when the federal Centers for Disease Control and Prevention celebrated "Ten Great Public Health Achievements in the 20th Century," its first and last reasons for celebrating "family planning" concerned unintended pregnancy.[4] In other words, the federal voice is concerned primarily to enable a woman to achieve her will regarding becoming pregnant. Advocacy for free choice regarding

---

[3] Don S. Browning, "Modern Law and Christian Jurisprudence on Marriage and Family," *Emory Law Journal* 58 (2008): 35–36.

[4] US Centers for Disease Control, "Achievements in Public Health, 1900–1999: Family Planning," *Morbidity and Mortality Weekly Report* 48, no. 47 (December 3,1999): 1073–1080.

the number and spacing of children is important, but quite different from advocating for children's welfare in connection with their family structure. Insofar as many but certainly not all nonmarital births are "unintended," the category of "unintended births" overlaps considerably with the category of "nonmarital" births; still, it does not cover it, nor is it framed as advocacy for channeling births into marriage. This is a classic example of prioritizing adults' interests.

Furthermore, the federal government is well aware that rates of nonmarital pregnancy have skyrocketed, and rates of unintended births have either increased, or remained the same – depending upon the source consulted – during the years of the most ambitious federal birth control programs. In the United States, non-marital births as a percentage of all births have risen from 3.8 percent in 1940, to five percent in 1960, to about eighteen percent in 1980, to thirty-three percent in the mid-1990s, to over forty percent in 2013, where they hover today.[5]

Reliable measures of unintended pregnancy are more difficult to find. They are disputed because minds change, partners disagree, time alters memories, and various researchers count different situations and outcomes as "unin-tended." For example, some count "mistimed" pregnancies or pregnancies ending in abortion as "unintended." Measures also vary between the two most prominent sources, the Centers for Disease Control and the Guttmacher Institute – a research and interest group promoting legal and widely available contraception and abortion in the United States. Guttmacher tends to report far higher rates of unintended pregnancy, likely because they add numbers of abortions to women's own reports of a pregnancy's "intendedness." No matter which source is used, however, it is clear that rates of unintended pregnancy have not significantly improved since the federal government's extensive con-traception programs began in the 1970s. Guttmacher, for example, reports that thirty-five percent of pregnancies were unintended in 1972,[6] fifty-seven percent in 1987, forty-nine percent in 1994,[7] fifty-one percent in 2001, and that rates remained flat or edged a bit higher through 2006.[8] A 2016 Guttmacher

5   Carmen Solomon-Fears, *Nonmarital Births: An Overview*, Congressional Research Report 7-5700, R43667, July 30, 2014, 8.
6   Christopher Tietze, "Unintended Pregnancies in the United States, 1970–1972," *Family Planning Perspectives* 11 (1979): 186–188,186 n.*.
7   John S. Santelli et al., "The Measurement and Meaning of Unintended Pregnancy," *Perspectives on Sexual and Reproductive Health* 35 (March/April 2003): 94–101.
8   Stanley K. Henshaw, "Unintended Pregnancy in the United States," *Family Planning Perspectives* 30 (1998): 24–29; Lawrence B. Finer and Stanley K. Henshaw, "Disparities in Rates of Unintended Pregnancy in the United States, 1994 and 2001," *Perspectives on Sexual and Reproductive Health* 38 (2006): 90–96.

publication puts unintended pregnancies at forty-five percent in 2011.[9] The Centers for Disease Control puts the rates of unintended pregnancy at thirty-nine percent in 1988, thirty-five percent in 2002, thirty-seven percent between 2006 and 2010, and thirty-four percent between 2011 and 2013.[10]

A report commissioned by the federal government from the Institute of Medicine – a nongovernmental organization regularly tapped to advise the government on health matters – concluded in 2011 that "there has been no major progress in the prevention of unintended pregnancy in light of the lack of decrease in rates over time and in comparison with rates in other countries."[11] The federal government is aware that about eighty-nine percent of sexually active women use contraception, and that rates of use have increased dramatically since the 1970s.[12]

As described in greater detail in Chapter Three, there are numerous reasons for these results, including imperfect design or use of contraception, as well as women's aversion to some forms of it. Cost is not generally cited as a factor, and indeed rates of unintended pregnancy are highest among poorer women who receive contraception free or at very low cost. Another possibility is that the physical, psychological and cultural separation of sex and children has influenced a relationship market more conducive to nonmarital sex, and even what is sometimes called in sociological literature "nonrelationship sex," or "casual sex." These behaviors may also have helped to decapacitate couples for the work of stable marriage and childbearing. I will treat this at greater length in Chapter Three.

The observation that contraception has facilitated more nonmarital sex is a commonplace in both scholarly and popular literature. This is not equivalent to an accusation that any particular sex education or contraception program will lead to a specific, traceable rise in sexual activity. It is rather a reference to the historically observed rise in nonmarital sex and acceptance of nonmarital sex, which followed widespread adoption of the pill and other modern contraceptives. The relationship between the two is observed by self-described

[9] Lawrence B. Finer and Mia R Zolna, "Declines in Unintended Pregnancy in the United States, 2008–2011," *The New England Journal of Medicine* 374 (2016): 843–852.

[10] US Centers for Disease Control, *Intended and Unintended Births in the United States: 1982–2010*, by William D. Mosher, et al., US Centers for Disease Control, National Health Statistics Report 55 (July 24, 2012), Table 1. Trends in the intendedness of births at conception, by marital status at birth and Hispanic origin and race of mother: United States, selected years.

[11] Institute of Medicine, *Women's Health Research: Progress, Pitfalls and Promise* (Washington, DC: National Academies Press, 2010), 143.

[12] US Department of Health and Human Services, *Use of Contraception in the U.S.: 1982–2008*, by William D. Mosher and Jo Jones, US Department of Health and Human Services (2010): 5, 9.

conservatives and liberals, and by experts across a wide range of disciplines. Secular humanist and socialist Paul Blanshard wrote in 1973: "[B]lessed be the pill! Perhaps some future historian will hail it as our century's greatest contribution to happiness – and also to the dissolution of Christian monogamy."[13] Sociologist Andrew Cherlin judges that it "has allowed young women and men to become sexually active long before they think about marriage."[14] And Nobel Prize winning economist George Akerlof, together with his wife, Federal Reserve Chair Janet Yellen and another economist, concluded that: "the norm of premarital sexual abstinence all but vanished in the wake of the technology shock."[15]

Since the 1970s, Americans' opinions on nonmarital sex have also changed considerably. According to a 2015 study in the *Archives of Sexual Behavior*, the percentage of Americans who hold the view that premarital sex "is not wrong at all" moved from twenty-nine percent (thirty-five percent of men and twenty-three percent of women) in the 1970s, to forty-two percent in the 1980s, and to fifty-five percent in the 2010s (fifty-nine percent of men and fifty-two percent of women).[16]

When the government regularly adopts the perspective that "unprotected sex makes babies," as distinguished from the fact that "sex makes babies," the link connecting sex and parenthood is verbally attenuated. The partners' responsibility for creation is either attenuated, or they are severely to "blame." If "unprotected sex" creates life, then it is the parent's failure (the failure to use technology), or it is technology's failure (to work properly), which creates new life. It is not the parents' sex that is directly linked to the making of a child. The language of "responsibility" is absent.

This effect – of separating adults from their responsibility for making new life – is potentially exacerbated when the government associates child-free adult sexual expression with goods that stir the blood of twentieth and twenty-first century human beings: freedom, identity-creation and equality. Sometimes dignity, personhood, destiny and autonomy are also added to the list. I will show that the federal government made these associations – in a ringing voice – especially in various Supreme Court decisions concerning contraception, abortion and same-sex marriage. These associations reinforce the impression

[13] Paul Blanshard, *Personal and Controversial: An Autobiography* (Boston: Beacon Press, 1973), 113.
[14] Andrew Cherlin, "American Marriage in the Early Twenty-First Century," *The Future of Children* 15 (2005): 49.
[15] George Akerlof, Janet L. Yellen and Michael L. Katz, "An Analysis of Out-of-Wedlock Childbearing in the United States," *The Quarterly Journal of Economics* 111 (1996): 309.
[16] Jean M. Twenge, Ryne A. Sherman and Brooke E. Wells. "Changes in American Adults' Sexual Behavior and Attitudes, 1972–2012," *Archives of Sexual Behavior* 44 (May 2015): 2273–2285.

that if a child is nevertheless conceived against adults' wishes, some right has been violated. Adult responsibility is not called to mind.

No matter the reasons for contraception's persistent and long-run failure to prevent nonmarital births, given how long it has failed, it is fair to conclude that the federal government's contraception policies do not demonstrate adequate attention to child welfare, especially in the context of the government's simultaneous attachment to valorizing adult sex, indifferent to marriage.

Third, I am not arguing that the federal government is actively inviting casual, nonmarital liaisons completely unmindful of children. I am not arguing that its policies are the equivalent of "if it feels good, do it" – although occasionally the government or its partners come surprisingly close to this line.

I am pointing out, however, that the government explicitly links consensual adult sexual expression with profound human goods, while regularly remaining agnostic to the partners' marital status. Furthermore, it does not use similarly emotional or emphatic language about the good of providing children stable, marital parents, except – and ironically – within the Supreme Court's same-sex marriage opinions, where the children involved will be separated from their biological mother or father or both, in every case.

I should note here a few occasions in which the federal government links adults' sexual expression with responsibility to children, even though I believe these are swamped by contrary messages. On its healthcare websites for teens, the federal government has mentioned disadvantages that teen parents' nonmarital children may suffer. It has also funded some sex education programs for teens which support sexual abstinence, and which include the message – among many others directed to self-care and social expectations – "that bearing children out-of-wedlock is likely to have harmful consequences for the child, the child's parents, and society."[17]

For a brief period between 2006 and 2008, the federal Department of Health and Human Services targeted abstinence messages to individuals in their twenties, as well as to teens. The effort was greeted with derision by the leadership of the (then-named) National Campaign to Prevent Teen Pregnancy and other groups, on the grounds that it was doomed to failure, or that matters concerning adults' sex lives were a matter of privacy, or that birth control was the better message and solution.[18]

---

[17] US Department of Health and Human Services, "State Abstinence Education Grant Program Fact Sheet," Family and Youth Services Bureau (April 28, 2015), www.acf.hhs.gov/fysb/resource/aegp-fact-sheet.

[18] Sharon Jayson, "Abstinence Message Goes Beyond Teens," *USA Today*, October 30, 2006 (updated October 31, 2006), www.usatoday.com/news/washington/2006-10-30-abstinence-messagex.htm.

The federal Healthy Marriage Initiative and Responsible Fatherhood programs[19] fund a variety of marriage education programs, including programs offered in high schools, or for unmarried individuals of any age. The great bulk of the program has been directed, however, to already pregnant or parenting couples and married couples. In 2004, the Department of Health and Human Services made available on its website a research paper entitled "A Comprehensive Framework for Marriage Education,"[20] which contained valuable information for prospective marriage educators, including those addressing unmarried audiences. A few states adopted high school programs, although not all continued them. Some of the high school programs have been evaluated. Reviewers have found small but positive effects, and expressed disappointment that the courses were elective and not mandatory.[21] Federal marriage program evaluations do not devote attention to high school or other individual marriage or relationship education efforts, but it seems likely that one or more of the high school programs includes discussion of the benefits for children of marital parenting.

From this review it is clear that the federal government rarely takes the opportunity to link the value of sexual expression both to marriage and to care for children. It would seem that, when it does, it is largely speaking to teens, not adults, or to already pregnant or parenting individuals. This book is concerned with its speech to unmarried adults, however, who account for eighty-five percent of nonmarital births. To this audience, the federal message is sexual expressionist.

Fourth, it should be obvious that I am not claiming that federal opinions about sexual expression are solely responsible for creating the environment and practices we have today – only that they have played a role. Our current situation has many "parents." Technology, entertainment, religion, philosophies, and other disciplines and movements played important roles. I will discuss the interplay between these sources and federal law and policy at the end of this chapter.

---

[19] US Department of Health and Human Services, Healthy Marriage and Responsible Fatherhood, Office of Family Assistance, www.acf.hhs.gov/ofa/programs/healthy-marriage.

[20] Alan J. Hawkins et al., *A Comprehensive Framework for Marriage Education, a report prepared for the Administration for Children and Families*, U.S. Department of Health and Human Services (2004), www.acf.hhs.gov/sites/default/files/opre/comp_framework.pdf.

[21] Vicki Larson, "Should Schools Teach Teens How to be Good Spouses?" *The Huffington Post*, August 16, 2012, www.huffingtonpost.com/vicki-larson/can-you-teach-kids-how-to_b_1272122.html; Sarah Halpern-Meekin, "High School Relationship and Marriage Education: A Comparison of Mandated and Self-Selected Treatment," *Journal of Family Issues* 32 (2011): 394–419, www.journals.sagepub.com/doi/pdf/10.1177/0192513X10383944; Scott P. Gardner et al., "Evaluation of the Connections Relationships and Marriage Curriculum," *Family Relations* 53 (2004): 521–527.

A fifth and final preliminary matter. A critique of sexual expressionism is not a denial that there is an important relationship between human sexual expression and health and happiness, for both women and men. Sexual relationships are important sources of personal happiness and of physical and emotional health.[22] Physical, psychological or social sexual dysfunctions are serious problems meriting care and treatment. Sex is a non-substitutable way of communicating love and solidarity, among other things. It displays and can further union. It is also the locus of the creation of nearly every human being (assisted reproductive technology is the other), and human society, beginning with the family. It would demean adult sexual partners to treat sex as strictly about procreation. Sexual partners are not procreative tools, but persons for whom sex is regularly an important and meaningful act, psychologically, emotionally and even spiritually. American society is well shot of ideas that sex – especially for women – is tawdry or unfit for reflection or affirmation.

A focus on the good of sexual expression was clearly required when it emerged toward the beginning of the twentieth century. At that time, it was determined that an unhealthy denial of the intrinsic good of sex, for both men and women, was harming especially the potential for companionate marriages.[23] The emergence of a response led to many healthy conclusions about, *inter alia*, the harm of the double standard, and the intrinsic good of the human body and the body–mind connection.

The federal government's affirmation of the good of individual sexual expression without children was likely a move to align itself with all of the positive features of our society's developing appreciation for sexual health, for women and for LGBT persons. Yet it is possible to acknowledge these noble impulses while criticizing the government's emphasis on adults' individual interests while leaving children insufficiently protected.

With sex, one is always dealing with a source of intense personal pleasure and meaning, prone to self-dealing, and simultaneously capable of originating a vulnerable child and his or her family structure. Both critics and enthusiastic supporters of new sexual freedoms understand the risks. The founder of Harvard University's Department of Sociology, Pitirim Sorokin, wrote as early as 1956 about how a focus in the sexual arena upon the individual satisfaction of each partner could strengthen the natural selfishness built into sex and

---

[22] See Linda J. Waite and Kara Joyner, "Emotional and Physical Satisfaction with Sex in Married, Cohabiting, and Dating Sexual Unions: Do Men and Women Differ?" in *Sex, Love, and Health in America: Private Choices and Public Policies*, ed. Edward O. Laumann and Robert T. Michael (Chicago: The University of Chicago Press, 2001): 239–274.

[23] Steven Seidman, *Romantic Longings: Love in America, 1830–1980* (New York: Routledge, 1993), 65–85.

reduce its being "tempered by mutual devotion and love."[24] Historian Steven Seidman cautions that, alongside the new goods of choice, pleasure, and new "types of collective life" made possible by sexual freedom, there were also the risks of destabilizing bonds, reducing people to means of pleasure, and confounding sexual communication.[25]

With these distinctions and clarifications completed, I now turn to a description of the federal government's sexual expressionism posture. I begin with the Supreme Court, the most prolific and emphatic author of sexual expressionism.

SEXUAL EXPRESSIONISM AT THE COURT

Beginning in 1972 with *Eisenstadt v. Baird*[26] – the decision granting single persons a constitutional right to access contraception – the US Supreme Court issued a series of decisions on contraception, abortion and same-sex relations, tending toward sexual expressionism. It was not until 2003, however, in the case of *Lawrence v. Texas*[27] (overturning a criminal homosexual sodomy ban), that the Court formally constitutionalized sexual expression outside of marriage, severed completely from procreation and indifferent to the marital status of a couple. In other words, *Lawrence* fully realized the sexual expressionist import of the earlier cases, and arrived after many of them. The potential for a constitutional interest in sexual expression separate from marriage, however, inhered all along in the contraception and abortion cases. It was there in *Eisenstadt's* separating sex from children and marriage both *de facto* and *de jure*. *De facto* because the Court's granting single persons' a right to separate sex from pregnancy facilitated sex without marriage. *De jure* because the terms in which a single person's right to contraception was granted – the right to make decisions about matters "fundamentally affecting a person,"[28] especially concerning childbearing – suggested a right to *decide* on sex without marriage. At the very least, it put the focus squarely on the adults' sexual expression, and not on the link between sex and children, or sex and marriage.

Before discussing additional sexual expression decisions, it is important to consider the constitutional doctrine in which the Court has embedded sexual expressionism: "substantive due process." This is because the characterization of a behavior as a "substantive due process right" is a way that the Supreme

---

[24] Pitirim A. Sorokin, *The American Sex Revolution* (Boston: Porter Sargent, 1956): 6.
[25] Seidman, *Romantic Longings*, 193–202.
[26] Eisenstadt v. Baird, 405 U.S. 436 (1972).
[27] Lawrence v. Texas, 539 U.S. 558 (2003).
[28] *Eisenstadt*, 453.

Court expresses its understanding that a behavior is essential to human freedom as we understand it in the United States. By characterizing sexual expression, or preventing pregnancy or birth following sex, as a "substantive due process" right, the Supreme Court elevates the human significance of these decisions. It indicates that they are essential to human freedom. My claim that the Court is "valorizing" sexual expression is therefore closely tied up with its use of a substantive due process framework in cases involving or facilitating sex without children and indifferent to the partners' marital status.

Substantive due process rights, and the Court's various tests for discerning these, are controversial. Since at least *Mugler v. Kansas,*[29] however, the Due Process Clause of the Fourteenth Amendment ("nor shall any State deprive any person of life, liberty, or property, without due process of law") has been understood to contain a "substantive" component, and not simply a guarantee of *procedural* fairness. The *substantive* guarantee "'bar[s] certain government actions regardless of the fairness of the procedures used to implement them'."[30] The modern inquiry by which an interest is assessed to determine whether it qualifies as a substantive due process right indicates why a positive conclusion carries so much cultural significance. Justice White in his dissent in the abortion case *Thornburgh v. Planned Parenthood*, describes this inquiry as follows:

> One approach has been to limit the class of fundamental liberties to those interests that are "implicit in the concept of ordered liberty" such that "neither liberty nor justice would exist if [they] were sacrificed." ... Another, broader approach is to define fundamental liberties as those that are "deeply rooted in this Nation's history and tradition."[31]

The plurality opinion in the 1992 abortion decision *Planned Parenthood v. Casey* added that substantive due process adjudication "has represented the balance which our Nation, built upon postulates of respect for the liberty of the individual, has struck between that liberty and the demands of organized society."[32] A later iteration of the manner in which the Court discerns a substantive due process right appeared in the 1998 assisted suicide decision *Washington v. Glucksberg*[33] when the Court said:

> Our established method of substantive due-process analysis has two primary features: First, we have regularly observed that the Due Process Clause

---

[29] Mugler v. Kansas, 123 U.S. 623 (1887).
[30] Planned Parenthood v. Casey, 505 U.S. 833, 847 (1992) (citation omitted).
[31] Thornburgh v. American College of Obstetricians and Gynecologists, 476 U.S. 747, 790 (1986) (White, J., dissenting).
[32] *Casey*, 850.
[33] Washington v. Glucksberg, 521 U.S. 702 (1997).

specially protects those fundamental rights and liberties which are, objectively, "deeply rooted in this Nation's history and tradition," ... ("so rooted in the traditions and conscience of our people as to be ranked as fundamental"), and "implicit in the concept of ordered liberty," such that "neither liberty nor justice would exist if they were sacrificed," ... Second, we have required in substantive due-process cases a "careful description" of the asserted fundamental liberty interest.... Our Nation's history, legal traditions, and practices thus provide the crucial "guideposts for responsible decisionmaking," ... that direct and restrain our exposition of the Due Process Clause.[34]

I turn back now to the Court's application of substantive due process analysis in the contraception and other cases. In *Eisenstadt*, the Court held that the "right of privacy" was a strand of substantive due process, and included single persons' right to decide to use contraception. Said the Court:

> If under *Griswold [v. Connecticut]*[35] the distribution of contraceptives to married persons cannot be prohibited, a ban on distribution to unmarried persons would be equally impermissible.... [T]he marital couple is not an independent entity with a mind and heart of its own, but an association of two individuals each with a separate intellectual and emotional makeup. If the right of privacy means anything, it is the right of the individual, married or single, to be free from unwarranted governmental intrusion into matters so fundamentally affecting a person as the decision whether to bear or beget a child.[36]

Eisenstadt was the foundation of sexual expressionism in a way that *Griswold v. Connecticut* was not, because it was the first to contemplate and facilitate sexual expression without concern for the marital status of the couple. In *Griswold*, the Court discovered a constitutional right of married persons to access contraception.

On its face *Eisenstadt's* language granting constitutional status to decisions about matters "fundamentally affecting a person," could have far broader purchase. Many, many personal decisions can be said to fundamentally affect a person. But *Eisenstadt* has not been extended to the vast majority of these decisions – for example, decisions about matters such as killing oneself,[37] or about an interest in obtaining an adequate education, or work at a living wage, or a safe place to live. And while the right of privacy has been interpreted to include the right to remain employed while pregnant

[34] Washington v. Glucksberg, 720, 721 (citations omitted).
[35] Griswold v. Connecticut, 381 U.S. 479 (1965).
[36] *Eisenstadt*, 453.
[37] Vacco v. Quill, 521 U.S. 793 (1997); *Washington v. Glucksberg*.

or childrearing,[38] it is far more frequently applied to protect acts connected with *not* bearing children – contraception, abortion and same-sex sexual relations and marriage – rather than acts directed to bearing them. All of this highlights by distinction how *Eisenstadt*, and later sexual expression cases relying upon substantive due process, were focusing more upon the right to avoid childbearing following sex, than they were about "fundamentally" important decisions in any general sense.

Eisenstadt also began the Supreme Court's articulation that substantive due process rights encompassed citizens' choices to shape or constitute their identity or personhood. *Eisenstadt* did this by characterizing the single person's decisions about sex and childbearing as matters "fundamentally affecting a person" in his or her "intellectual and emotional makeup." This aspect of "liberty" – decisions intellectually or emotionally "making up" a person – appeared again, strengthened, in the later abortion decision, *Casey*. It also appeared in the three homosexual sex or marriage cases.

One year after *Eisenstadt*, in *Roe v. Wade*[39] the Court extended the substantive due process right of privacy to include the right to obtain a legal abortion. The Court permitted states to regulate or even proscribe abortion during the last trimester of pregnancy, except where the mother's life or "health" was at stake, with health defined so as to include "all factors – physical, emotional, psychological, familial, and the woman's age – relevant to the wellbeing of the patient."[40] The portion of *Roe* which described the outcomes of refusing to recognize a right of abortion, linked abortion with a woman's ability to maintain happiness, psychological and physical health and social status, saying:

> The detriment that the State would impose upon the pregnant woman by denying this choice altogether is apparent. Specific and direct harm medically diagnosable even in early pregnancy may be involved. Maternity, or additional offspring, may force upon the woman a distressful life and future. Psychological harm may be imminent. Mental and physical health may be taxed by child care. There is also the distress, for all concerned, associated with the unwanted child, and there is the problem of bringing a child into a family already unable, psychologically and otherwise, to care for it. In other cases, as in this one, the additional difficulties and continuing stigma of unwed motherhood may be involved.[41]

---

[38] Cleveland v. LaFleur, 414 U.S. 632 (1974).
[39] Roe v. Wade, 410 U.S. 113 (1973).
[40] *Roe*, 192.
[41] *Roe*, 153.

Indicating the importance it ascribed to the abortion right, the *Roe* Court offered the following substantive due process analysis:

> The Constitution does not explicitly mention any right of privacy. In a line of decisions, however, going back perhaps as far as *Union Pacific R. Co. v. Botsford*, the Court has recognized that a right of personal privacy, or a guarantee of certain areas or zones of privacy, does exist under the Constitution.... These decisions make it clear that only personal rights that can be deemed "fundamental" or "implicit in the concept of ordered liberty," ... are included in this guarantee of personal privacy. They also make it clear that the right has some extension to activities relating to marriage, ... procreation, ... contraception, ... family relationships, ... and child rearing and education.... This right of privacy, whether it be founded in the Fourteenth Amendment's concept of personal liberty and restrictions upon state action [i.e., substantive due process], as we feel it is, or, as the District Court determined, in the Ninth Amendment's reservation of rights to the people, is broad enough to encompass a woman's decision whether or not to terminate her pregnancy.[42]

Like *Eisenstadt*, *Roe* and later abortion decisions did not explicitly announce a right to sexual expression free of children and indifferent to marriage, but clearly advanced the case for sexual expressionism, both *de facto and de jure*. *De facto* by reducing fears about the personal, social and legal repercussions of nonmarital sex and even pregnancy. *De jure* by linking sex without children to the notion of women's freedom and to earlier and constitutionally robust rights to marriage, family relationships and child-rearing.

A corollary of sexual expressionism was sounded in the abortion cases, beginning with *Roe*: the disparaging of pregnancy and childbirth. The Court linked both of these with physical, psychological and mental harm, with the burdens of childcare, with countermanding an adult's will respecting childbearing, and with stigma. This is not to deny that there is sacrifice, and even distress, potentially associated with pregnancy or an unwanted child. It is rather to observe that the Court paints an unrelentingly negative picture. Nothing is said about any of the possible goods of parenting or human life, or the possibility that the mother might be happy in the short- or long-run to have a child she did not will, or to have avoided abortion and any feelings of post-abortion regret some women suffer.

The next abortion decision to significantly advance sexual expressionism was *Planned Parenthood of Southeastern Pennsylvania v. Casey*. *Casey* reaffirmed the constitutional right of abortion, while demoting abortion to

[42] *Roe*, 152–153.

a "liberty interest" under substantive due process, and announcing a more deferential test for evaluating abortion laws. At the same time, *Casey* more explicitly linked sex – without childbirth and indifferent to the partners' stability – with a woman's ability to be free, equal to men, happy and empowered to form her own identity. The Court's tone was passionate.

Linking sex-without-childbirth to women's freedom, the *Casey* Court wrote that abortion is a "response to the consequence of unplanned activity [sex] or to the failure of conventional birth control."[43] It continued: "for two decades of economic and social developments," women "have organized intimate relationships and made choices that define their views of themselves and their places in society, in reliance on the availability of abortion in the event that contraception should fail."[44] Specifying further what it meant by the link between legal abortion, equality and women's self-identity, the Court added that "[t]he ability of women to participate equally in the economic and social life of the Nation has been facilitated by their ability to control their reproductive lives."[45] It then linked these claims to substantive due process in its most famous passage:

> These matters, involving the most intimate and personal choices a person may make in a lifetime, choices central to personal dignity and autonomy, are central to the liberty protected by the Fourteenth Amendment. At the heart of liberty is the right to define one's own concept of existence, of meaning, of the universe, and of the mystery of human life. Beliefs about these matters could not define the attributes of personhood were they formed under compulsion of the State.[46]

To deny an abortion right, said *Casey*, was tantamount to the State "insist[ing] ... upon its own vision of the woman's role."[47] With abortion, the very "destiny" of the woman was at stake and it "must be shaped to a large extent on her own conception of her spiritual imperatives and her place in society."[48] After citing its contraception cases, the Court wrote that both its contraception and its abortion decisions are about a woman's liberty because they involve "personal decisions concerning not only the meaning of procreation but also human responsibility and respect for it."[49]

---

[43] *Casey*, 856.
[44] *Casey*, 835.
[45] *Casey*, 853.
[46] *Casey*, 851.
[47] *Casey*, 852.
[48] Ibid.
[49] *Casey*, 853.

While *Casey*'s soaring language is certainly subject to varying interpretations, at the very least it can be said that it firmly linked women's ability to avoid childrearing following sexual intercourse (in or out of marriage) with her interest in forming her personal identity.

Like *Roe*, *Casey* also sounded a note of antipathy to childbearing, and by extension to children, although it also recognized some citizens' deep respect for the lives of unborn children. The Court wrote: "the liberty of the woman is at stake in a sense unique to the human condition, and so, unique to the law." "The mother who carries a child to full term is subject to anxieties, to physical constraints, to pain that only she must bear." "Her suffering is too intimate and personal for the State to insist, without more, upon its own vision of the woman's role, however dominant that vision has been in the course of our history and our culture."[50] At the same time, the Court did sound a note of respect for children, referring to abortion as involving "not only the meaning of procreation but also human responsibility and respect for it." It referred to the pro-life view as "based on such reverence for the wonder of creation."[51]

The Court's decision in *Gonzales. v. Carhart*,[52] – a "partial birth abortion" decision – recognized *Casey* as controlling law, but avoided dwelling upon the burdens of childbearing or equating abortion with women's freedom and equality. Instead – and likely as a response to what it called a "gruesome" abortion procedure (crushing, then evacuating the head of a nearly-delivered child) – the Court focused upon legislatures' ability to regulate the medical profession.

The Court's 2016 opinion in *Whole Woman's Health v. Hellerstedt*,[53] however, reversed course again and dwelt upon the importance to women of convenient abortion access. The Court struck down Texas' laws requiring abortion doctors to have certain hospital admitting privileges, and requiring abortion clinics to meet ambulatory surgical center standards. The Court concluded that the regulations placed a "substantial obstacle" in the path of a woman seeking an abortion, because they might reduce the number of abortion clinics to the point that women would have to travel too far, and would receive less "individualized attention, serious conversation and emotional support" in connection with their abortions.[54]

The Supreme Court decisions above associated women's childfree sexual expression with values such as freedom, equality, spiritual imperatives, destiny,

---

[50] *Casey*, 852.
[51] *Casey*, 853.
[52] Gonzales v. Carhart, 550 U.S. 124 (2007).
[53] Whole Woman's Health v. Hellerstedt, 136 S. Ct. 2292 (2016).
[54] *Hellerstedt*, 2318.

overcoming past discrimination and achieving identity. These are *per se* profound matters. As further discussed below, they also resonated with cultural values and idea gaining strength especially during the second half of the twentieth century. This is an important aspect of what I term the "valorization" of sexual expression.

While pre-*Casey* decisions facilitated nonmarital sexual expression free of children, it was *Casey* itself which first took constitutional cognizance of "intimate choices" and "unplanned activity" free of children, on the grounds that sex is identity- and personhood-shaping. *Lawrence v. Texas* took the next step, explicitly appearing to articulate a constitutional right to sexual expression unlinked to marriage and children – with exceptions only for "injury to a person or abuse of an institution the law protects."[55] The two same-sex marriage opinions, *United States v. Windsor*,[56] and *Obergefell v. Hodges*,[57] thereafter relied heavily upon *Lawrence*.

Before taking up *Lawrence, Windsor* and *Obergefell*, a few words about how cases concerning intrinsically nonprocreative sex are related to nonmarital births among heterosexuals, the subject of this book. These three cases are included because each of them – like the abortion and contraception cases – supported individual interests in sexual expression without any link to procreation, and in *Lawrence* also without a link to marriage. All used emotional language to valorize nonprocreative sexual activities, claiming that they were identity-, dignity- and personhood-shaping. These three cases therefore elevated the legal status of nonprocreative sex by analogy to the cases securing nonprocreative heterosexual intercourse. In a sense, they valorized nonprocreative sexual intercourse more strongly than the cases involving heterosexuals because the sexual activities before the Court were *inevitably* nonprocreative, yet protected to the same degree and by means of similar language about their importance to freedom, happiness, equality, and identity. Interestingly, sociologist Anthony Giddens observed in 1992 that the separation of sex from reproduction would eventually lead to an improved status for homosexuality given how, with contraception, sex was finally separated entirely from the "exigencies of reproduction."[58]

In *Lawrence*, the Court struck down a Texas law criminalizing homosexual sodomy (oral or anal sex) and held that "individual decisions concerning the intimacies of physical relationships, even when not intended to produce

---

[55] *Lawrence*, 567.
[56] United States v. Windsor, 133 S. Ct. 2675 (2013).
[57] Obergefell v. Hodges, 135 S. Ct. 2584 (2015).
[58] Anthony Giddens, *The Transformation of Intimacy: Sexuality, Love, and Eroticism in Modern Societies* (Stanford: Stanford University Press, 1992): 27–28.

offspring, are a form of 'liberty' protected by due process."[59] Citing *Casey's* emotional passage on the meaning of liberty, the Court reasoned that homosexual sexual acts are a core aspect of a person's "right to define one's own concept of existence, of meaning, of the universe, and of the mystery of human life." Immediately following this quotation, the Court reasoned that "[p]ersons in a homosexual relationship may seek autonomy for these purposes just as heterosexual persons do."[60] As further evidence of the law's high regard for the nonprocreative sex of single persons, the Court relied for its holding upon prior constitutional cases upholding married couples' constitutional right to determine the number and spacing of children, and to control their children's education. Putting nonmarital sodomy – sex closed to children and apart from marriage – on the same constitutional plane as the marital and procreative sex adjudicated in these earlier cases, the Court then opined in *dicta* that "[w]hen sexuality finds overt expression in intimate conduct with another person, the conduct can be but one element in a personal bond that is more enduring."[61]

Both of the same-sex marriage opinions, *Windsor* and *Obergefell*, also affirm the Supreme Court's adoption of sexual expressionism. They assign crucial importance to nonprocreative sexual conduct, and link it with foundational human values such as freedom, equality and dignity. They rely upon *Lawrence* and the contraception cases a great deal for the claim that the Constitution protects a couple's moral and sexual choices. They put sexual acts which can produce children on the same plane with sexual acts which cannot. As a new feature of the sexual expression cases, they normalize the separation of children from one or both of their biological parents by forbidding states to take a special interest in sexual pairs who might procreate and rear their own biological children, as distinguished from sexual pairs whose children – should they have custody of any – will in every case be separated from their mother or father, or both.

This disappearance of marriage's role as a tool for encouraging potentially procreative pairs to have and rear marital versus nonmarital children is a significant milestone. It is the opposite end of the spectrum from laws that had punished adults or children for nonmarital childbearing, or conduct that might lead to it. Following the disappearance of laws concerning fornication, cohabitation, adultery and illegitimacy – all of which had attempted to advance marital versus nonmarital parenting – there were no legal sticks left; but there was a carrot – marriage. Following *Obergefell*, there are no longer

---

[59] *Lawrence*, 577 (citation omitted).
[60] *Lawrence*, 574.
[61] *Lawrence*, 567.

even any legal carrots directed specifically to potentially procreative pairs, although there remain social and cultural incentives for opposite-sex couples to choose marriage as a parenting context.

Looking first at *Windsor*, the Court there struck down a portion of the Defense of Marriage Act, thus requiring the federal government to recognize same-sex marriages licensed by any state. *Windsor* (albeit in *dicta* following its statement that marriage recognition is strictly a state law matter) defined marriage recognition as a state's "acknowledgment of the intimate relationship between two people."[62] The majority opinion was replete with language pronouncing that giving marriage recognition to intimate pairs is a crucial aspect of acknowledging their "dignity," "equality," "destiny" and "personhood."

The *Windsor* Court relied heavily upon *Lawrence* for its holding. Its reasoning is tortuous but it appears that *Windsor* first assumed (from the *dicta* in *Lawrence*) that sex always "form[s] one element in a personal bond that is more enduring." Thus, when a state granted marriage recognition to sexually intimate same-sex pairs it was according "far-reaching legal acknowledgement" of a couple's equal dignity with enduring, and constitutionally valorized relationships: opposite-sex marriages.[63] The Defense of Marriage Act's ban on federal recognition of such a marriage therefore denied a same-sex couple equal dignity, and could only be based on a "bare congressional desire to harm a politically unpopular group."[64] Noteworthy here is the amount of importance *Windsor* attributes to sex. Though casual sex is a well-known fact, *Windsor* clothes every sexual encounter with great importance. It is *always* "one element in a personal bond that is more enduring." Notice further how *Windsor* elevates all intrinsically nonprocreative, sexually active pairs to what had previously been known as marriage – ordinarily procreative pairs. Both moves imply that adult sexual choices – not procreation or children – merit tremendous constitutional concern.

Obergefell v. Hodges, the Supreme Court opinion creating a constitutional right to same-sex marriage, also performed important work to valorize sexual expression unlinked to children. While the Court was not indifferent to the stability of the couple (the same-sex couple who wished to marry), its judgment was orthogonal to the stability of the mother and father who procreate a child. At the same time, the Court facilitated the separation of children from their mother or father, by requiring states to grant marriage to desiring same-sex pairs, who could now more often, and more easily, pursue adoption or

---

[62] *Windsor*, 2692.
[63] *Windsor*, 2692–2693.
[64] *Windsor*, 2693 (citation omitted).

assisted reproductive technologies. The Court smoothed the way for separating children from their biological parents, ironically enough, by claiming that its marriage precedents regularly described marriage's "varied rights" – including establishing a home and bringing up children – as a "unified whole."[65] In other words, it suggested that the right of same-sex marriage included a right to "bring[] up children," at the very same moment that it held that states were acting irrationally if they decided to define marriage on the basis of the goods of procreation and of childrearing by a child's natural mother and father.

Furthermore, and ironically enough for a marriage opinion, *Obergefell* advanced sexual expressionism by stressing the sexual rights and interests of the *individual*. This occurred very likely because the Court approached the subject of same-sex marriage from the perspective of the history of discrimination against homosexual individuals, which discrimination was often based upon repugnance at their sexual acts. This led the Court to conclude that being excluded from marriage to a partner of one's choice demeaned a person's individual dignity on the basis of his or her sexual practices. The very first "relevant precedent" the *Obergefell* Court cited to support its judgment was the "concept of individual autonomy."[66] The Court then claimed that the "fundamental liberty" at stake included an individual's right to make "intimate choices [sex] that define personal identity and beliefs."[67] It called marriage an "intimate right" of "individual ... self-definition" which also shapes "an individual's destiny."[68] It highlighted the individual's interest in marriage recognition in one of its most famous, impassioned passages: "Marriage responds to the universal fear that a lonely person might call out only to find no one there."[69]

Obergefell was sexual expressionist, not only in its focus upon the adult individuals involved, but also because of the way in which it emphasized the importance of sex to the individual, and because of the links the ruling made with sexual choices: choices which are closed to procreation but allegedly crucial to individual identity formation. All of this it then identified with marriage, giving flesh to Anthony Giddens' observation that separating sex from children would remake marriage. The word would be the same, but it would be a shell containing new contents.[70]

---

[65] *Obergefell*, 2600.
[66] *Obergefell*, 2599.
[67] *Obergefell*, 2597.
[68] *Obergefell*, 2599.
[69] *Obergefell*, 2600.
[70] Giddens, *The Transformation of Intimacy*, 58, 135, 154.

The choice before the *Obergefell* Court was binary. Until *Obergefell*, children were embedded in the constitutional understanding of the fundamental right of marriage, and the vast majority of states' marriage recognition statutes. From 1879 forward, case after case before the Supreme Court clearly demonstrated that the birth of children and the securing of children's wellbeing, alongside adults' interests in companionship and intimacy, *together* provided the rationale for denominating marriage a fundamental Due Process right, and for recognizing states' compelling interests in their marriage recognition laws.[71] After *Obergefell*, a state's interest in the birth of children, and children's interests in remaining linked to their biological mother and father, *cannot* ground any state's marriage recognition law.

Some might insist that *Obergefell* attended to children's interests in the portion of the opinion wherein the majority claimed that its decision rested in part on the need to "safeguard[] children and families" because "[w]ithout the recognition, stability, and predictability marriage offers, their children suffer

---

[71] See e.g., Reynolds v. United States, 98 U.S. 145, 165 (1879) ("Upon [marriage] society may be said to be built."); Murphy v. Ramsey, 114 U.S. 15, 45 (1885)("'marriage' – a term traditionally understood by this Court, like everyone else, to mean 'the union for life of one man and one woman'."); Zablocki v. Redhail, 434 U.S. 374, 384, 386 (1978) (describing "marriage" as "fundamental to the very existence and survival of the race," and vindicating the right to "marry and raise the child in a traditional family setting."); *Loving v. Virginia*, 388 U.S. 1, 12 (1967) ("Marriage is ... fundamental to our very existence and survival."); Skinner v. Oklahoma ex rel. Williamson, 316 U.S. 535, 541 (1942) ("Marriage and procreation are fundamental to the very existence and survival of the race."); Meyer v. Nebraska, 262 US. 390, 399 (1923) (The right to "marry, establish a home and bring up children ... [is] essential to the orderly pursuit of happiness by free men."); Bowers v. Hardwick, 478 U.S. 186, 216 (1986) (Stevens, J., dissenting) (marriage is a "societal license to cohabit and to produce legitimate offspring."). Until Obergefell, the Court's opinions stressed how marriage fosters adults' responsibility for forming the next generation of citizens. In Lehr v. Robertson, 463 U.S. 248, 257 (1983) for example, the Court refused to treat an unmarried father identically to a married father with respect to rights respecting his biological child, stating that "marriage has played a critical role ... in developing the decentralized structure of our democratic society. In recognition of that role, and as part of the overarching concern for serving the best interests of children, state laws almost universally express an appropriate preference for the formal family." In other marriage opinions the Court highlighted the advantages of blood ties for turning parents toward their children See, e.g. Parham v. J.R., 442 U.S. at 602 ("historically [the law] has recognized that natural bonds of affection lead parents to act in the best interests of their children."); Smith v. Organization of Foster Families for Equality and Reform, 431 U.S. 816, 844 (1977) (families' "blood relationship" as part of the "importance of the familial relationship to the individuals involved and to the society." The Court also wrote that the "importance of the familial relationship, to the individuals involved and to the society, stems from the emotional attachments that derive from the intimacy of daily association,... as well as from the fact of blood relationship."); and Santosky v. Kramer, 455 U.S. 745, 758–59 (1982)("[A] natural parent's desire for and right to the companionship, care, custody, and management of his or her children ... is an interest far more precious than any property right.")

the stigma of knowing their families are somehow lesser. They also suffer the significant material costs of being raised by unmarried parents, relegated through no fault of their own to a more difficult and uncertain life."[72] A closer analysis, however, undercuts this claim.

First, there is the irony of the Court's strong endorsement of the benefits of married parenthood for children – *not* in the prior forty years of cases in which it facilitated nonmarital, heterosexual intercourse, but rather in a case involving children who will be separated from one or both biological parents in every single instance. The majority of children currently living in same-sex partner households were conceived in a prior heterosexual union involving one of the parties in the same-sex partnership, who is now parted from a former lover or spouse.[73] The remainder of the children will be separated from one or both parents by means of adoption or collateral (third party) assisted reproduction.

Second, the *Obergefell* court spoke as if there was certainty regarding whether children reared in same-sex-partner households will have outcomes comparable to children reared in opposite-sex married homes, or whether those children will derive benefits from states' recognizing the adults' relationship as marriage. The Court cited no literature regarding third-party benefits to children as a result of marriage between the same-sex adults in their household. Furthermore, the literature about children's welfare in same-sex homes was in disarray in 2015, and remains so today.[74] The literature about "stigma" is similarly quite uncertain.[75]

---

[72] *Obergefell*, 2472, 2600–2601.

[73] US Census Bureau, *Demographics of Same-Sex Couple Households with Children*, by Kristy M. Krivickas Daphne Lofquist, US Census Bureau (Working Paper No. 2011-11), www.census .gov/hhes/samesex/files/Krivickas-Lofquist%20PAA%202011.pdf; US Department of Health and Human Services, National Adoption Information Clearing House, www.childwelfare.gov/ pubPDFs/f_gay.pdf ("Defining the family structure of gay and lesbian parents can be a challenging task. The most common type of homosexual household is step or blended families. These are gay and lesbian parents who had their biological children in a former heterosexual relationship, then came out, and created a new family with another partner.")

[74] Loren Marks, "Same-sex parenting and children's outcomes: A closer examination of the American Psychological Association's brief on lesbian and gay parenting," *Social Science Research* 41 (2012): 735–751; Walter R. Schumm, "A Review and Critique of Research on Same-Sex Parenting and Adoption, *Psychological Reports*" 119 (2016): 641–760 (Reviewing all extant studies on same-sex parenting and child outcomes and concluding: "While some researchers have tended to conclude that there are no differences whatsoever in terms of child outcomes as a function of parental sexual orientation, such conclusions appear premature in light of more recent data in which some different outcomes have been observed in a few studies.")

[75] Mark Regnerus, "Is structural stigma's effect on the mortality of sexual minorities robust? A failure to replicate the results of a published study," *Social Science and Medicine*: (in press), www.dx.doi.org/10.1016/j.socscimed.2016.11.018.

The *Obergefell* Court was unwilling, however, to wait until more certain information about children's welfare was developed. Instead, it declared that there already existed "enhanced understanding of the issue" sufficient to conclude that states did not have interests in linking children with their own mother and father, which interests could be sufficient to overcome same-sex partners' interests in marriage recognition.[76] *Obergefell's* claim regarding children's enhanced wellbeing within married same-sex households, therefore, is better grasped as an attempt to find some familiar strand of constitutional family law on which to base a newly created right, and not as a move to protect children.

Conduct Equals Identity?

There is one further line of reasoning which has led to the current practice of linking sexual expression without children and indifferent to marriage with substantive due process protections for "identity formation." This is the notion introduced by the *Lawrence* Court that disapproval of any consensual sexual act is equivalent to disapproval of the people who undertake it, which disapproval can also render a law irrational and therefore illegal. This is a legally and philosophically consequential move. It identifies an entire person according to his or her sexual acts.

Justice Kennedy's majority opinion adopted this line of thought in *Lawrence*, stating: "When homosexual conduct is made criminal by the law of the State, that declaration in and of itself is an invitation to subject homosexual persons to discrimination."[77] His majority opinion in *Windsor* made the same connection. It stated that the Defense of Marriage Act's refusal to recognize same-sex marriages – which he defined as sexual behavior plus commitment between two people – could only flow from a "bare ... desire to harm" people.[78]

The *Christian Legal Society v. Martinez* decision,[79] citing *Lawrence*, also conflated sexual identity and conduct. The Christian Legal Society – unlike any prior student group at the University of California (Hastings College of Law) – was denied official recognition, on the ground that it would not accept as members students who rejected its core beliefs. While the society admitted "all comers" into membership, in line with university policy, it denied leadership roles to those who violated Christian sexual teachings and refused

---

[76] *Obergefell*, 2605.
[77] *Lawrence*, 575.
[78] *Lawrence*, 580.
[79] Christian Legal Society v. Martinez, 561 U.S. 661 (2010).

to feel repentance. The Christian Legal Society contended that it was not excluding individuals from membership in its law school chapter because of sexual orientation (an exclusion that would have violated university policy) but rather "on the basis of a conjunction of [immoral gay or straight sexual] conduct," as evaluated by Christian beliefs, "and the belief that the conduct is not wrong."[80] The Supreme Court refused to draw the line between conduct and identity, however, saying, "[o]ur decisions have declined to distinguish between status [sexual orientation identity] and conduct in this context."[81] For this proposition it cited *Lawrence.*

Although the Supreme Court has weighed in on elements of sexual expressionism in other cases, these contributions were not as significant as those recounted above. I turn now to the roles of the other two branches of the federal government in voicing sexual expressionism.

SEXUAL EXPRESSIONISM AND THE EXECUTIVE AND LEGISLATIVE BRANCHES

There are several ways in which the executive and legislative branches have forwarded sexual expressionism over approximately the past half-century. The administration of Barack Obama was almost certainly the most explicitly supportive of sexual expressionism, but actions of prior administrations have also adopted this theme from time to time.

Contraception Programs

Birth control programs and messaging are important paths by which the executive valorizes sexual expression. While federal birth control programs have a long history, it appears that their stated purposes have migrated toward sexual expressionism, while also retaining their intentions to prevent births especially to the very young and to the poor. Earlier federal programs were more openly targeted to the poor. Current efforts remain so targeted in fact and in funding, but are accompanied by additional efforts and language extolling the goods of contraception for women of every socioeconomic level. It is not overstating matters to say that at the present time, a politician's vocal support for any legal measure supporting contraception has become a "proxy" or a "dog whistle" for his or her position on adult women's freedom generally, including sexual freedom unlinked to marriage.

---

[80] *Christian Legal Society,* 689.
[81] Ibid.

The following material very briefly recounts the history of federal contraception efforts in order to understand by distinction the language it uses today regarding the goals of its contraceptive programs.

The federal Centers for Disease Control credits the movement to make contraception part of government policy to Margaret Sanger, the foundress of the Planned Parenthood Federation of America. In the 1920s and 30s, Sanger wrote about the health advantages of spacing childbirth, limiting family size and avoiding abortion.[82]

Contraception was first federally funded in the early 1940s, when Margaret Sanger persuaded Eleanor Roosevelt that it could combat venereal disease and help to avoid pregnancies among women working to supply the war effort.[83] Later, when the federal government stepped up its birth control activities in the 1960s, it was responding to overpopulation fears and concerns about early and frequent childbearing, especially among the poor.[84] Then as now, federal efforts faced resistance from some African American leaders worried about what they labeled genocidal targeting.[85]

The Johnson administration expanded federal family planning funding especially on a platform of poverty reduction in the 1960s and created family planning centers within the National Institutes of Health, and what is now called the Department of Health and Human Services ("HHS").[86]

Under the Nixon Administration, the argument for subsidizing family planning was based upon a desire to reduce childbearing by lower-income Americans. It was also proposed that a family with fewer children could invest more in each one.[87]

With strong support from Republicans, Congress passed Title X of the Public Health Service Act in 1970. Title X provides significant amounts of federal funding to states for contraception.

Today, the federal government spends nearly 2.1 billion dollars annually on birth control, with the lion's share allocated to programs serving lower-income Americans. About seventy-five percent of all federal spending is through Medicaid – the federal health insurance program for poor Americans – and

---

[82] See US Centers for Disease Control, *Achievements in Public Health, 1900–1999*.
[83] William L. Davis, "Family Planning Services: A History of U.S. Federal Legislation," *Journal of Family History* 16 (1991): 381–400, 385.
[84] *Id.* at 386.
[85] Ibid.
[86] William L. Davis, "Family Planning Services," 396, 387.
[87] Martha J. Bailey, "Fifty Years of Family Planning: New Evidence on the Long-Run Effects of Increasing Access to Contraception," Brookings Papers on Economic Activity (Spring, 2013): 341–409, www.ncbi.nlm.nih.gov/pmc/articles/PMC4203450/.

ten percent is through Title X. Annually, states spend approximately 225 million dollars more.[88]

The federal framing of its rationale for spending has changed. One does not hear any longer about overpopulation and reducing the numbers of poor children, or about maintaining women's ability to work in any area of the economy in which the government has a vested interest. The language is rather about avoiding unintended pregnancy, and is often paired with claims about health problems for mothers or children claimed to be linked to a pregnancy's unintendedness.

Federal messages today also unmistakably communicate that birth control is a crucial aspect of women's freedom, and their ability to attain social equality with men. As the federal Centers for Disease Control wrote in its 1999 account of major achievements in public health, contraception has "improved the social and economic role of women."[89]

The women's freedom message underlies the government's phrasing of its primary goal for contraception programs: preventing "unintended" pregnancies – that is, pregnancies women do not will. It is the first and last goal noted in the Centers for Disease Control's 1999 summary of the country's progress in family planning.[90] The scientific body on which HHS often relies for expert advice – the Institute of Medicine – also continually states that family planning's first goal is the reduction of unintended pregnancy.[91]

To argue that this message is sexual expressionist is not to disagree that women should be able to freely determine the number and spacing of their children. It is rather to point out that when the government indifferently proposes the good of avoiding unintended pregnancy as between married and single women, and does not speak about children's welfare simultaneously, the government is at least suggesting indifference regarding nonmarital childbirth which is willed or intended.

Another series of events pointing toward a sexual expressionist cast to the government's contraception efforts was the Affordable Care Act's "contraception

---

[88] Guttmacher Institute, "Publicly Funded Family Planning Services in the United States: Fact Sheet" (September 2016), www.guttmacher.org/sites/default/files/factsheet/fb_contraceptive_serv_0.pdf.

[89] US Centers for Disease Control, *Achievements in Public Health, 1900–1999*.

[90] Ibid.

[91] Institute of Medicine, "A Review of the HHS Family Planning Program: Mission, Management, and Measurement of Results," ed. Adrienne Stith Butler and Ellen Wright Clayton, *Institute of Medicine: Committee on a Comprehensive Review of the HHS Office of Family Planning Title X Program*, (Washington, DC: National Academies Press, 2009), www.ncbi.nlm.nih.gov/books/NBK215219/.

mandate," and the accompanying language and behavior of its federal advocates and partners.

The Affordable Care Act ("ACA") became law in 2010. It contained a "preventive health care" provision, the specific contents of which were to be fleshed out by the HHS. As they have done on prior occasions, HHS turned to the Institute of Medicine. The Institute of Medicine empaneled a committee composed largely of medical personnel associated with Planned Parenthood and other contraception and abortion advocates.[92] The report recommended that all health insurance policies be required to cover all Food and Drug Administration-approved contraceptives without any co-pay. HHS freely acknowledged that the language of "contraceptives" included drugs and devices that could act to destroy an already developing human embryo.[93] HHS adopted the recommendation that became known as the "contraception mandate." It was promoted as solving the problem of women's higher health costs, and promoting both women's and children's health by reducing unintended pregnancy. It was also regularly and forcefully advanced as securing women's freedom and equality.

The mandate exempted churches, but religious institutions such as hospitals, schools and charities were required to file paperwork with the government which had the effect of triggering governmental action attaching contraception coverage to the employer's insurance plan. Over 100 lawsuits involving more than 300 plaintiffs were filed against the federal government. The government took two trips to the Supreme Court – in *Burwell v. Hobby Lobby Stores, Inc.*[94] and *Zubik v. Burwell*[95] – which handed victory or near victory to both sets of conscientious objectors. Following *Zubik*, HHS continued to seek a way to attach contraception to the religious institutions' policies. It is likely, however, at the time of writing, that a 2017 Trump administration executive order will be interpreted to direct HHS not to enforce the mandate against religious institutions.

The federal government demonstrated robust attachment to sexual expressionist ideas in several ways throughout the mandate controversy. One indication was certainly its willingness to pursue the Little Sisters of the Poor as

---

[92] Americans United for Life, "Letter from Anna Franzonello, Americans United for Life, to Centers for Medicare and Medicaid Services" (September 29, 2011), www.aul.org/wp-content/uploads/2014/10/Americans-United-for-Life-October-2014-HHS-Final-Rule-Comment.pdf.

[93] 26 Code of Federal Regulations 54.9815–2713(a)(1)(iv)(2013); 29 Code of Federal Regulations 2590.715–2713(a)(1)(iv)(2013); 26 Code of Federal Regulations 54.9815–2713(a)(1)(iv)(2013).

[94] Burwell v. Hobby Lobby, 134 S.Ct. 2751 (2014).

[95] Zubik v. Burwell, 136 S.Ct. 1557 (2016).

long and as aggressively as it did. The Little Sisters were an enormously popular charity providing care to the elderly poor. During oral argument before the Supreme Court, the Solicitor General of the United States stated that the government held the highest level of interest – a "compelling interest" – in religious institutions' being required to provide free contraception. He also insisted that the government would not be satisfied for an employee to receive free contraception if she had to carry a second insurance card to obtain it.[96] Years after the litigation had begun, and even after the Supreme Court had ordered the federal government to find less intrusive ways to deliver contraception to the sisters' employees, the government continued to stall and to seek ways to enforce the mandate.

Second, HHS and the Department of Justice, in their public and in their litigation arguments in favor of the mandate, regularly insisted that it would achieve women's "equal status as healthy and productive members of the job force."[97] At no time did they draw any distinction between married and single women, or note the correlation of federal contraception programs with higher rates of nonmarital and unintended births, especially among poorer women receiving federally funded contraception at no cost. At some points, the government linked intended pregnancy (speaking always about the individual woman, without reference to marriage) with a longer list of goods: "her health, her child's health, and the economic wellbeing of herself and her family."[98]

A third aspect of the mandate evidencing the government's adoption of sexual expressionism was the weakness of its economic or health rationales. This highlights how much weight the "women's freedom" argument was required to bear. The government continually asserted that contraception was the most important source of women's higher health care costs. In fact its own sources showed that health care cost differentials between men and women arose not from contraception, but due to costs that the mandate did not reimburse. To wit: women's longevity, their greater predisposition to visit doctors and their childbearing, cause women's overall higher lifetime costs.[99]

---

[96] *Zubik v. Burwell*, Oral Argument Transcript, www.supremecourt.gov/oral_arguments/ argument_transcripts/14-1418_1bn2.pdf, page 87, lines 6–7, and page 83, lines 2–18.

[97] 77 Code of Federal Regulations 8725, 8728 (2013).

[98] Reply Brief for the Petitioners, *Sebelius v. Hobby Lobby Stores, Inc., et al.*, (United States Supreme Court, No 13–354), 46.

[99] Centers for Medicare and Medicaid Services, *National Health Care Spending by Gender and Age, 2004 Highlights* (2004), www.cms.gov/Research-Statistics-Dataand-Systems/Statistics-Trends-andReports/NationalHealthExpendData/downloads/2004GenderandAgeHighlights .pdf; US Centers for Disease Control, Visits to physician offices, hospital outpatient departments, and hospital emergency departments by age, sex, and race: United States, selected years 1995–2011 (2012); US Centers for Disease Control, Expenses for health care and

Fourth, prior to the contraception mandate, calls for free contraception in every health care plan were commonly made by contraception and abortion interest groups such as the Guttmacher Institute and Planned Parenthood. In fact, the Guttmacher Institute had earlier called for a contraception mandate[100] using the same language ultimately adopted by the federal government. There was no grass roots advocacy by women for such a benefit. The mandate was rather spearheaded by the federal government with strong support from its partners at Guttmacher and Planned Parenthood.

Fifth, there was not a significant shortfall in the availability or use of birth control by women prior to the mandate. The government acknowledged that over eighty-nine percent of sexually active women were using birth control already.[101] Guttmacher's sources showed that only a tiny percent of women reported that they could not afford contraception pre-mandate.[102] These women were almost certainly eligible for government programs and benefits already providing contraception free or on a sliding-scale (see the Medicaid discussion below). The employed, more middle-class women targeted by the mandate to receive free contraception, were not complaining about its cost. Most were already insured for it.[103] Not surprisingly, five years after the mandate was introduced, the Guttmacher Institute acknowledged that it failed to produce greater use of contraception by sexually active women.[104]

Sixth, the government's argument that contraception could benefit women's health by reducing unintended pregnancies was highly controversial. As described above, unintended pregnancies did not decrease following the growth of federal funding for contraception in the early 1970s; and they increased precisely among the groups – low income women – receiving it free or at very low cost. Women without a free contraception benefit have

---

prescribed medicine, by selected population characteristics: United States, selected years 1987–2010 (2012).

[100] Adam Sonfield, "The Case for Insurance Coverage of Contraceptive Services and Supplies Without Cost-Sharing," *Guttmacher Policy Review* 14 (2011): 7.

[101] US Department of Health and Human Services, *Use of Contraception in the U.S.: 1982–2008*, 5, 9.

[102] See Helen M. Alvaré, "No Compelling Interest: The 'Birth Control' Mandate and Religious Freedom," *Villanova Law Review* 58 (2013): 427–430.

[103] Institute of Medicine, *Clinical Preventive Services for Women: Closing the Gaps* (Washington, DC: The National Academies Press, 2011), 108–109; see also Alvaré, "No Compelling Interest: The 'Birth Control' Mandate and Religious Freedom," 427–439.

[104] Jonathan Bearak and Rachel K. Jones, "Did Contraceptive Use Patterns Change After the Affordable Care Act?: A Descriptive Analysis" (The Guttmacher Institute: Women's Health Issues) (March 2017), https://www.guttmacher.org/article/2017/03/did-contraceptive-use-patterns-change-after-affordable-care-act-descriptive-analysis.

lower rates of unintended pregnancy.[105] Even during the period of time when twenty-six states began enforcing various types of contraception mandates upon local health insurance providers, unintended pregnancy rates in those states stayed the same, or may have even increased slightly.[106]

The government's argument about the relationship between unintended pregnancy and women's health was also very incomplete. Most of the studies it relied upon spoke only of "correlation" not "causation," and also noted the possibility of reverse causation between the claimed health "effects" of unintended pregnancy – violence, drinking, smoking, depression and unintended pregnancy – and unintended pregnancy itself. Some sources suggested that a third factor – a higher taste for risk – could account both for the unintended pregnancy and the named health conditions. Furthermore, the government's health argument never fully reflected the widely acknowledged health risks of hormonal contraception, or the reality that women with health conditions strongly contraindicating for pregnancy are usually advised to avoid hormonal contraceptives.[107] Finally, it is significant that the US Preventive Services Task Force – the highest federal expertise on the subject of "preventive care" – has not, even to this day, recommended contraception as preventive health care for women.[108]

Seventh, in their advocacy for the mandate, members of Congress, the White House, and HHS and its private partners, relied heavily upon the arguments of single women about the need for free contraception for sex without fear of pregnancy. At the dawn of the mandate, a Planned Parenthood official published an editorial in the *New York Times* stating that the mandate would enable her divorced daughter to afford more expensive birth control.[109] On a National Public Radio program on which I appeared, a representative of the National Women's Law Coalition praised the mandate because it could pay for her single daughter's long acting contraception.[110]

Eventually, certain members of Congress, the White House and HHS chose Sandra Fluke – a single law student attending Georgetown University law school – to be the public face of the mandate. Ms. Fluke argued at a specially

---

[105] Guttmacher Institute, "Unintended Pregnancy in the United States: Fact Sheet" (September 2016), www.guttmacher.org/fact-sheet/unintended-pregnancy-united-states.

[106] Michael J. New, "Analyzing the Impact of State Level Contraception Mandates on Public Health Outcomes," *Ave Maria Law Review* 13 (2015): 345–369.

[107] Alvaré, "No Compelling Interest," 411–417.

[108] US Preventive Services Task Force, Published Recommendations, www.uspreventiveservices taskforce.org (current as of January 2017).

[109] Vanessa Cullins, "Make Birth Control Affordable," *The New York Times*, July 18, 2011, A23.

[110] National Public Radio, "New Debate Over Contraceptives and Women's Health," *The Diane Rehm Show*, July 21, 2011, www.thedianerehmshow.org/shows/2011-07-21/new-debate-over-contraceptives-and-womens-health.

convened congressional hearing and later in the news media, that her dignity and freedom as a woman obligated her religiously affiliated law school to buy her contraception in order for her to have sex with her boyfriend without the risk of pregnancy. After Rush Limbaugh called her a "slut" on his radio program, President Obama publicized that he had telephoned her to express his personal gratitude for her statements,[111] and his assurances that her parents would be proud of her. Thereafter, she was the face of women's freedom at "women's night" at the Democratic National Convention renominating Barack Obama for president. Ms. Fluke thereafter transitioned into full-time work within the Obama campaign, speaking continually about the mandate.

Another public face closely associated with the Obama administration's message on contraception was Hollywood actress Lena Dunham. On behalf of the Obama candidacy, Ms. Dunham filmed a re-election advertisement promoting the mandate, and comparing voting for Obama to a first sexual experience. She closed with the suggestion that it's "super uncool to be out and about and someone says, 'Did you …' and you say 'No I wasn't ready'" – oddly appearing to advocate nonmarital sex for even a conflicted woman or girl.[112]

The Obama campaign, the secretary of HHS and various members of Congress began to refer to conscientious objectors or critics of Planned Parenthood as waging a "war on women."[113] In short, advocacy for the mandate or for contraception became a proxy for supporting women. This politicized leveraging of contraception made no reference whatsoever to the good of linking sex with a concern for marital childbearing. Presidential campaign postcards rather urged women to "vote like your lady parts depend on it … because they kinda do,"[114] and invented a "letter to home" from a young, single adult, asking her parents for[115] "$18,000 to help pay for my birth control?"– referring

[111] Lucy Madison, "Obama calls Sandra Fluke to offer support over Limbaugh comments," *CBS News* (March 12, 2012, 9:54 AM), www.cbsnews.com/news/obama-calls-sandra-fluke-to-offer-support-over-limbaugh-comments/.

[112] Lena Dunham, "Your First Time," YouTube video, www.youtube.com/watch?v=o6G3nwhPuR4.

[113] Emily Schultheis, "Why Democrats Are Ditching the 'War on Women'," *The Atlantic*, July 31, 2014, www.theatlantic.com/politics/archive/2014/07/why-democrats-are-ditching-the-war-on-women/457929/.

[114] Daniel Halper, "Obama Campaign: 'Vote Like Your Lady Parts Depend on it. Because they kinda do,'" *The Weekly Standard*, October 2, 2012, www.washingtonpost.com/blogs/fact-checker/post/misleading-messages-from-obama-campaign-on-contraceptive-mandate/2012/10/04/ebb2148c-0cdf-11e2-bd1a-b868e65d57eb_blog.html.

[115] Josh Hicks, "Misleading messages from the Obama campaign on the contraceptive mandate," *The Washington Post*, October 5, 2012, www.washingtonpost.com/blogs/fact-checker/post/misleading-messages-from-obama-campaign-on-contraceptive-mandate/2012/10/04/ebb2148c-0cdf-11e2-bd1a-b868e65d57eb_blog.html.

to the claim that Republican candidate Mitt Romney would repeal the health care law and the mandate. The political use of the "war on women" extended into the 2014 campaigns. One candidate in particular, Mo Udall, used contraception so often as a proxy for his "pro-woman" stance, that the media eventually crowned him "Mark Uterus."[116]

Abortion

Abortion is related to sexual expressionism for the same reason that contraception is: because it separates sex from children and can lower the psychological and practical barriers to nonmarital sex. Contraception does not accomplish this separation perfectly because it fails regularly, or women forget it or choose not to use it. Over fifty-one percent of women seeking abortions reported using contraception in the month they became pregnant.[117] Only abortion definitively separates sex from children.

As described above, the Supreme Court's *Casey* decision made this very clear when it linked women's right to abortion to their interest in pursuing "unplanned activity" which might result in pregnancy, which in turn could interfere with personal or economic plans.

Executive power respecting abortion has been far more curtailed than respecting contraception. This is due largely to various laws banning federal spending or protecting conscientious objection regarding abortion.[118] Such restrictions have existed since shortly after *Roe v. Wade* created a constitutional right to abortion in 1973, and have persisted more or less in similar form until today.

Still, the Obama Administration championed legal abortion more readily than any prior administration. Over time it abandoned the language used by the administration of Bill Clinton about abortion being "safe, legal and rare." Instead, President Obama adopted the language of "choice" and of a "core constitutional right" assuring that "daughters have the same rights, freedoms, and opportunities as our sons."[119] Give that it is possible for a

---

[116] Carl M. Cannon, "Obama, Udall and What 2014 Was Really About," *The Denver Post*, November 9, 2014, www.realclearpolitics.com/articles/2014/11/09/obama_udall_and_what_2014_was_really_about_124604.html.

[117] Guttmacher Institute, "Induced Abortion in the United States: Fact Sheet," January, 2017.

[118] See, e.g., 42 U.S.C. § 300a-7 (The Church Amendment, 1973); § 507(d) of Title V of Division H of the Consolidated Appropriations Act, 2016, Pub. L. No. 114-113 (Hyde/Weldon Conscience Protection Amendment).

[119] Dave Boyer, "Obama 'deeply committed' to preserving abortion rights," *The Washington Times*, January 22, 2015, www.washingtontimes.com/news/2015/jan/22/obama-deeply-committed-preserving-abortion-rights/.

woman to be a parent of a born child, *and* to have equal rights, freedoms and opportunities with men, it appears that the President was reasoning that abortion is an essential element of women's freedom and equality, on the grounds that women, like men, should be able to avoid childbirth following sex.

The Obama and Clinton administrations intervened regularly in the Supreme Court on the side of greater access to abortion. President Obama also used his executive powers to issue orders and allow agency rulemaking forwarding legal abortion explicitly in terms of women's rights. One of President Obama's very first acts as President, for example, was to overturn the "Mexico City Policy," thus to allow federal money to flow to organizations overseas which also promote or provide abortions with their own funds. On his third day in office, President Trump reversed the Mexico City Policy, also by executive order.

President Obama also warmly endorsed legal abortion in a personal manner, stating that while children should be taught not to treat sex "casually," if a young woman were to become pregnant – including his own daughters – he would not "want them punished with a baby."[120] The suggestion is that unintended children are a punishment for sex.

Perhaps the boldest example of executive authority supporting abortion in women's rights terms was a July 2016 HHS rule "Nondiscrimination in Health Programs and Activities" claiming to implement section 1557 of the Affordable Care Act.[121] This regulation banned sex discrimination by various federal programs and grantees, defining it to include discrimination based upon a "termination of pregnancy." The rule offered no religious or other conscientious exemptions. It makes clear that the federal government proposes that there is a complete overlap between the rights of women and the right to ensure that sex does not result in childbirth.

Agency Fact Sheets

Another way in which the federal executive promotes sexual expressionism is through publicly available "factsheets" on sex published by executive agencies. Speaking both to single and married women over twenty (the largest cohort of women experiencing nonmarital births) about deciding to have a

---

[120] The Brody Files Blog, "Obama Says He Doesn't Want His Daughters Punished with a Baby," blog entry by David Brody, March 31, 2008, www.blogs.cbn.com/thebrodyfile/archive/2008/03/31/obama-says-he-doesnt-want-his-daughters-punished-with-a.aspx?mobile=false.

[121] 81 Fed. Reg. 31,375 (May 18, 2016).

child – the federal website womenshealth.gov advises them that "if you are sexually active" "you should set some goals about having (or not having) children." "This is called a reproductive life plan ..." and "[y]our personal values and beliefs will help you make your plan."[122] Nothing is said about parents' responsibility for creating their children's family structure, or the on-average superior prospects of children in marital families.

The Obama administration's White House Council on Women and Girls further signaled its indifferent stance toward nonmarital births via a report it issued in 2011.[123] Under the heading of continuing "problems" for women, one could find the subjects of wage and income equity, poverty, unique health challenges, and intimate partner violence. When it came to the report's assertions, however, that "[f]ewer women are married," or "single-mother households are more common than single-father" households, or that there are "reshaped patterns in marriage and divorce," the report says only that these phenomena "affect women and men differently." The normative language of "progress" or "problems" was absent, and only neutral descriptive language was used.

Furthermore, HHS has a set of goals entitled "Healthy People 2020," with advice to teens about avoiding "unintended pregnancy" and derailing their future. A few, brief lines speak bluntly about how *teen* pregnancy can harm a child: "children of teen parents are more likely to have lower cognitive attainment and exhibit more behavior problems;" "[s]ons of teen mothers are more likely to be incarcerated, and daughters are more likely to become adolescent mothers."[124]

The advice to adult women, however, is entirely without mention of children's welfare, focusing instead on adults' wishes. "Providers should encourage patients to develop a reproductive life plan." "A reproductive life plan is a set of goals and action steps based on personal values and resources about whether and when to become pregnant and have (or not have) children."[125]

[122] US Department of Health and Human Services, *Before you get pregnant* (February 1, 2017), www.womenshealth.gov/pregnancy/before-you-get-pregnant/sexually-active.html#pubs.

[123] US Dept. of Commerce, Executive Office of the President and White House Council on Women and Girls, *Women in America: Indicators of Social and Economic Wellbeing* (2011), www.whitehouse.gov/sites/default/files/rss viewer/Women in America.pdf (accessed January 29, 2017).

[124] US Department of Health and Human Services, *Healthy People 2020: Family Planning*, www.healthypeople.gov/2020/topics-objectives/topic/family-planning.

[125] Ibid.

Federal Partnerships

The federal government partners with many private organizations, especially as grantees, in connection with sexual expression and contraception. Planned Parenthood is likely the closest federal partner on the question of sexual expression, and is both the largest single distributor of contraception and the largest provider of abortion in the United States. The federal government funds Planned Parenthood a great deal in order for it to provide contraception to the public. According to a letter from the United States Government Accountability Office to Congress in 2015,[126] Planned Parenthood received 344 million dollars from the federal government in fiscal years 2010–12.[127]

Planned Parenthood has received generous federal grants under both Republican and Democrat administrations, but was exceptionally close to the Obama Administration. Planned Parenthood's political arm supported President Obama's reelection and he, in turn, became the first sitting president to directly address a Planned Parenthood meeting. There, he referred to himself as ""a president who's going to be right there with you, fighting every step of the way." He also characterized abortion restrictions in violent terms, as an "assault on women's rights" and characterized efforts against abortion as attempting to "turn back the clock" to the 1950s.[128] At the time of writing, the Trump administration has promised to redirect to other healthcare entities the federal money ordinarily granted to Planned Parenthood.

Following 2015 revelations of Planned Parenthood's willingness to negotiate the sale of fetal body parts obtained from abortion procedures, many states moved to cut off funding on the grounds of repugnance. In response, the Obama administration issued a regulation[129] threatening states with removal of all Title X funds if they "prohibit[ed] an entity from participating for reasons other than its ability to provide Title X services." States objecting to Planned

---

[126] Letter from Marcia Crosse, Director, Health Care, US Government Accountability Office, "Response to Congressional Requesters: Health Care Funding: Federal Obligations to and Expenditures by Selected Entities Involved in Health-Related Activities, 2010–2012" (March 20, 2015), www.gao.gov/assets/670/669140.pdf.

[127] *Id.*, 5.

[128] Associated Press, "Obama tells Planned Parenthood: abortion foes want return to 1950s," *Fox News*, April 26, 2013, www.foxnews.com/politics/2013/04/26/obama-tells-planned-parenthood-abortion-foes-want-return-to-150s.html.

[129] 42 Code of Federal Regulations Part 59.3 (b) (2016) ("Compliance with Title X Requirements by Project Recipients in Selecting Subrecipients"); see also Stephanie Armour, "States Warned Over Ending Medicaid Funds for Planned Parenthood," *The Wall Street Journal*, August 12, 2015, www.wsj.com/articles/hhs-warns-states-of-possible-violation-in-ending-medicaid-funds-for-planned-parenthood-1439392786?ru=yahoo?mod=yahoo_itp.

Parenthood had been giving Title X money to a variety of other health care providers who could provide birth control. In so many words, the regulation was meant to require states to provide Title X grants to Planned Parenthood against states' will.

Planned Parenthood has become a very straightforward advocate of sexual expression without attention to children's welfare or its links to marriage. It directly links both contraception and abortion with women's ability to live "strong healthy lives and fulfill their dreams – no ceilings, no limits."[130] To the extent that it is concerned about childbearing after sex, it is first and foremost about whether or not the woman's intention is served.

Even when advising teens, Planned Parenthood's "Am I Ready" information page suggests that, while a girl may wish to talk to a parent or other adult, "[y]ou – and only you – get to decide when you're ready to have sex." It further advises that, "[i]t's important to think about how having sex fits in with your health, values, school and career goals, relationships with others, and your feelings about yourself."[131]

Planned Parenthood's "Understanding Sexual Activity" information page for older women and men simply states that sex includes a "wide range of behaviors" and is for many "an important way to connect with ourselves and other people." On the subject of pregnancy, Planned Parenthood opines: "[n]o matter if you are married, partnered, or single, you have a lot to think about if you're considering getting pregnant and having a child. Only you can decide when the time is right for you."[132]

Specifically regarding parenting without a child, Planned Parenthood recommends that the reader ask herself questions that pertain exclusively to an adult's wishes:

> Like raising a child with a partner, raising a child alone can be exciting, rewarding, and challenging. One of the benefits of single parenting is that you do not have to compromise your values and beliefs with a partner. You can raise your child as you wish.

> If you are considering parenting without a partner, questions about money, career or school, support, and child care can be even more important. Will I have to put school or my career on hold to become a parent? Can I count on the support of family and friends? Will money be a problem? Can I afford

[130] Planned Parenthood, "About Us," www.plannedparenthood.org/about-us/who-we-are#sthash .FYjEBf6z.dpuf (accessed January 3, 2017).

[131] Planned Parenthood, "Am I Ready?," www.plannedparenthood.org/teens/sex/am-i-ready (accessed January 3, 2017).

[132] Planned Parenthood, "Considering Pregnancy," www.plannedparenthood.org/learn/pregnancy/ considering-pregnancy#sthash.L7uUJMbb.dpuf (accessed January 3, 2017).

child care? Is there someone I trust to take care of my child if I have to stay late at work or school, or get sick?[133]

Planned Parenthood provides nothing for any of its audiences on the goods of linking sex and marriage for the welfare of children. Sex is rather characterized as all about the teen or adult partner's consent to a range of sexual activities, about self-development and feelings, and perhaps about connection with another human being. Since the *Griswold* case in 1965, Planned Parenthood is regularly the complainant in lawsuits seeking to overturn substantive or funding restrictions on birth control or abortion at any time during pregnancy, for any reason, and by any method.

The National Campaign to Prevent Teen and Unplanned Pregnancy (NCTUP) is another important federal partner. It receives significant grants from HHS. Its spokespersons and resources are offered to the public on federal websites. On HHS' website womenshealth.gov, NCTUP's Bedsider ("online birth control support") is promoted as a good guide to sexual relationships. A Bedsider representative is quoted there saying: "It's important to validate all different kinds of consensual sexual and romantic experiences."[134]

NCTUP was founded in 1996 to reduce teen pregnancies. Later, its mission was expanded to include reducing "unplanned" pregnancies among young adults. Nearly its entire mission can be summarized as: use contraception. It takes no position on abortion. Regarding sex, it is plainly sexual expressionist where adults are concerned.

NCTUP's projects are numerous and include, *inter alia*, outreach to colleges, communications campaigns including the Bedsider program, programs to insert messages into entertainment, and public policy and research.[135]

NCTUP's advice to teens can be appropriately cautious. "Can I get pregnant if ..." reads one Facebook post at their Stay Teen page. NCTUP's answer: "Hint: If you had sex, the answer is probably yes." It continues: "The reality is, men and women's bodies are designed to reproduce."[136]

[133] Planned Parenthood, "Considering Pregnancy: Parenting Without a Partner," www.planned parenthood.org/learn/pregnancy/considering-pregnancy#sthash.L7uUJMbb.dpuf (accessed January 3, 2017).

[134] US Department of Health and Human Services, "An Interview About Talking to Teens About Healthy Relationships and Sex: Kayla Smith," (Peer Health Educator at Bedsider), *Spotlight on Women's Health*, June 23, 2016, www.womenshealth.gov/blog/spotlight-kayla-smith (accessed February 1, 2017).

[135] The National Campaign to Prevent Teen and Unplanned Pregnancy, "What We Do," thenationalcampaign.org/about/what-we-do.

[136] Meg McDonnell, "All Sex All the Time: A campaign to prevent unplanned pregnancy encourages casual sex," *National Review*, March 6, 2014, www.nationalreview.com/article/372682/all-sex-all-time-meg-t-mcdonnell.

But its Bedsider.org messaging for all – with over ten million visitors since 2011 – does not advise readers to think about marriage as the best sexual context for children. Instead, Bedsider freely encourages casual sex for singles. It's "Frisky Friday" series, for example, offers recipes for "aphrodisiac food," or "heat[ing] up your weekends with our best sex tips." It offers consolation for girls depressed after nonrelationship sex saying, "[s]ome of the most modern, empowered, secure, sexylicious women among us have had at least one walk of shame."

NCTUP's e-cards and graphics have included invitations for casual sex, photos of natural objects resembling genitalia, or bondage equipment and other soft pornography.[137] Its "About Us" section touts a woman's right to "a happy, healthy sex life without worrying about an unplanned pregnancy." And it offers members a "Booty Log" app that encourages anonymous sharing of one's sexcapades in an online database. A Frisky Friday blog urged readers to cohabit and/or to have nonmarital babies with the advice:

> Being unmarried doesn't mean no babies, no home, no relationship, no sex, no carpools, and no happiness.... Create the life you want. You don't have to do anything except the stuff that pays the rent and makes you happy. If you want to have a kid, there are ways to do that.... And if you want to shack up without the formality of a marriage certificate, go for it. Just don't ever feel bad about your choice if you choose not to marry.
>
> If it's right for you, it's right.[138]

Planned Parenthood and NCTUP are the most prominent federal partners in the contraception or abortion spheres, empowered by federal dollars and encouragement. To the millions of women and men they touch, they plainly communicate a sexual expressionist message.

Gender and Sexual Expressionism

As noted above in the material concerning the *Lawrence*, *Windsor* and *Obergefell* cases, federal messaging about homosexual sex and marriage also speaks in a sexual expressionist voice. Governmental affirmation of homosexual sex and marriage affirms sexual expressionism in an important if partial

---

[137] National Campaign to Prevent Teen and Unplanned Pregnancy, Bedsider Photos, www .facebook.com/bedsider/photos/pb.131611470215125.-2207520000.1393271176./549424618433806/ ?type=3andtheater.

[138] The National Campaign to Prevent Teen and Unplanned Pregnancy, "The Real Housewives of Not In This Lifetime: What if marriage isn't your thing?" Frisky Fridays, March 15, 2013, www.bedsider.org/features/512-the-real-housewives-of-not-in-this-lifetime-what-if-marriage-isn-t-your-thing.

way to listeners. It valorizes the importance to the individual of sexual feelings and activities which are completely severed from the possibility of procreation. It links them to the creation of personal identity. This was treated at length, *supra*, in the discussion concerning the Supreme Court's same-sex relationship opinions.

The Obama administration was historically unique in its attention to sexual orientation and same-sex marriage. The president and vice-president reversed their longstanding opposition to same-sex marriage. Its Department of Justice claimed that it could not defend the Defense of Marriage Act on the grounds that no state could have even a rational reason for taking special interest in relationships between procreative pairs. The administration entered a brief on behalf of same-sex marriage in the *Obergefell* case, and when the *Obergefell* Court announced a right to same-sex marriage, the White House draped itself in the colored lights of the same-sex marriage movement. The President issued a ringing, emotional endorsement.[139] And the Vice-President soon after officiated a same-sex wedding at the White House.

In 2016, in a move again highlighting the administration's preoccupation with individual sexual identity and expression, a "Dear Colleague" letter from the Department of Justice Civil Rights Division[140] required public schools to allow students to use a bathroom of their choice. DOJ claimed that this constituted a valid interpretation of the word "sex" in Title IX of the Education Amendments of 1972, and claimed that a "student's gender identity [is] the student's sex for purposes of Title IX and its implementing regulations."

In late 2016 another federal agency, the U.S. Commission on Civil Rights, expressed its support for rights to contraception, abortion and same-sex marriage, while casting religious objectors in harshly negative terms. In its report, *Peaceful Coexistence: Reconciling Nondiscrimination Principles With Civil Liberties*,[141] the agency's chairman said that "[t]he phrases 'religious liberty' and 'religious freedom' will stand for nothing except hypocrisy so long as they remain code words for discrimination, intolerance, racism, sexism, homophobia, Islamophobia, Christian supremacy, or any form of intolerance.'"[142]

---

[139] Barack Obama, Remarks by the President on the Supreme Court Decision on Marriage Equality, June 26, 2015, www.whitehouse.gov/the-press-office/2015/06/26/remarks-president-supreme-court-decision-marriage-equality.

[140] US Department of Justice, Civil Rights Division, Dear Colleague Letter on Transgender Students, May 13, 2016, www.justice.gov/opa/file/850986/download.

[141] US Commission on Civil Rights, *Peaceful Coexistence: Reconciling Nondiscrimination Principles With Civil Liberties* (Briefing Report, September 2016) (Chairman Martin R. Castro Statement), p. 29, www.usccr.gov/pubs/Peaceful-Coexistence-09-07-16.PDF.

[142] *Id.* at 29.

A dissenting member of the commission accused the majority of vaulting sexual expressionism over religious freedom, writing that "secularism, holds an individual's unfettered sexual self-expression as a preeminent concern because it is an aspect of their self-creation."[143]

Male v. Female

Especially the judicial and executive branches of the federal government have, from time to time, cast suspicion upon men and the possibility of harmonious relationships between men and women. This is a small but important collateral aspect of the phenomenon I call sexual expressionism. In addition to separating sex from the idea of children, it stresses self-realization and autonomy versus mutuality between men and women. From time to time it even lapses into an emphasis on strife between men and woman. Perhaps the Supreme Court's biggest contribution on this point is in the way it dealt with husbands in the abortion cases, particularly in *Casey*. There the Court struck down Pennsylvania's law requiring a woman to notify (not to obtain the consent of) her husband before having an abortion – unless he was not the father, or the pregnancy was the result of his assault, or she had reason to believe that furnishing notice would lead to violence. Even with these exceptions, the Court held that men are so regularly violent that they could not be trusted to be notified that their wife intended to abort their offspring. To support its decision, the Court relied upon data which lumped together violence committed by any current or past, marital or nonmarital sexual partner a woman could have, under the heading "intimate partner violence." But it is known today, and it was known then, that husbands are far less violent to women than are men in other relationships or ex-relationships.[144] The *Casey* Court unfairly painted a very dark picture of marriage.

---

[143] The US *Commission on Civil Rights, Peaceful Coexistence: Reconciling Nondiscrimination Principles With Civil Liberties* (Commissioner Peter Kirsanow Statement), 42.

[144] *Casey*, 887–888; See, e.g., Martin Daly and Margo Wilson, "The 'Cinderella effect': Elevated Mistreatment of Stepchildren in Comparison to Those Living with Genetic Parents," www.cep.ucsb.edu/buller/cinderella%20effect%20facts.pdf; US Department of Justice, *Violence against Women: A National Crime Victimization Survey Report*, by Ronet Bachman, U.S. Department of Justice (Washington, D.C.,1994), www.ncjrs.gov/pdffiles1/Digitization/145325NCJRS.pdf; W. Bradford Wilcox, "#YesWomenAndChildren Are Safer Within Intact Marriages," *The Federalist*, January 6, 2015, www.thefederalist.com/2015/01/06/yesallwomenandchildren-are-safer-within-intact-marriages/; Janet Yuen-Ha Wong, et al., "A comparison of intimate partner violence and associated physical injuries between cohabitating and married women: a 5-year medical chart review," Biomedical Central Public Health 2016, DOI: 10.1186/s12889-016-3879-y.

Regarding the executive branch, while the Obama White House helpfully convened conferences, distributed information and lent rhetorical support to issues affecting women, it also displayed a tendency to emphasize divisions between the sexes. And it never spotlighted the good of cooperation and mutual support between women and men. Instead, there was a great deal of attention paid to subjects involving discord or even violence between men and women.

The websites of the White House Council on Women and Girls, of HHS or the Department of Justice, the Department of Labor, and of the Equal Employment Opportunity Commission, for example, referred regularly to executive interventions concerning: domestic violence, violence against indigenous women, unequal pay, rape, sexual assault on campuses, sexual assault in the military, "breaking down barriers," claimed higher costs of women's health care, the glass ceiling, women's underrepresentation in STEM jobs (science, technology, engineering and math), differences between the sexes' retirement readiness, and cultural changes for giving women the respect they deserve. Yet today, men and women are working side by side in almost every public and private sphere. There should be no shortage of insights and lessons about this new level of cooperation.

DOES THE FEDERAL POSITION MATTER?

The federal position on sexual expression is clear, but does it matter for children's wellbeing? Clearly, nonmarital parenting and its associated difficulties are not strictly a function of federal rhetoric, federal spending or even federal rules and constitutional rights. Yet the federal voice still plays an important role.

It can influence by way of public admiration for the president or his spokespersons. There is also the objectively powerful bully pulpit of elected officials, especially but not exclusively of the executive and his surrogates and agency directors. This is true, not only while elected officials are governing, but also during their election and re-election campaigns. During these periods, surrogates and supporters, including celebrities, donors, and interest groups, offer prominent defenses of a candidate's positions.

Furthermore, presidential speeches and web pages claim that presidential initiatives spur changes. And indeed, from time to time, states propose laws mirroring federal initiatives, following a president's lead. The Obama administration claimed that the president inspired legal and community action regarding women's issues and community college initiatives for the working poor.[145]

---

[145] See, e.g., The White House, Office of the Press Secretary, "White House Unveils America's College Promise Proposal: Tuition-Free Community College for Responsible Students,"

President George W. Bush intended his exhortations to unleash "armies of compassion." President Trump claims the power to "make things happen."

Research suggests that presidential influence may be heightened if the president uses particularly effective rhetoric, or if he focuses a great deal on particular images or issues.[146] This seems to be common sense.

Presidents also claim to effectively channel public sentiment. President Obama famously stated "[w]hen they won't act, I will. He claimed that America "can't wait for Congress to get its act together."[147] President Trump echoes these sentiments.

The President and members of Congress can also influence citizens by using the powers of their office to organize celebrities, entrepreneurs, philanthropists, and corporate leaders on behalf of various causes. In 2016, for example, the White House invited several thousand technology entrepreneurs to a luxury event showcasing American accomplishments. One entrepreneur told the press that the invitees understood that the President "wants to leave behind a 'nation of makers.'"[148] Similar public events involved the Secretary of State meeting with Hollywood filmmakers to urge collaboration against ISIS propaganda.[149]

Regarding the Supreme Court's influence in particular, some understand the Court as a "republican schoolmaster," promoting virtues among citizens via its power to say what the Constitution means.[150] The Court has a track record of positioning itself as the defender of the weak, not least often in its sexual expression opinions where women and LGBT citizens are identified as

January 9, 2015, obamawhitehouse.archives.gov/the-press-office/2015/01/09/fact-sheet-white-house-unveils-america-s-college-promise-proposal-tuitio; Ashley A. Smith, "Obama Steps up Push for Free Community College," *Inside Higher Education*, September 9, 2015, www.insidehighered.com/news/2015/09/09/obama-unveils-new-push-national-free-community-college.

[146] See James N. Druckman and Lawrence R. Jacobs, "Presidential Responsiveness to Public Opinion," in *The Oxford Handbook of the American Presidency* (Oxford: Oxford University Press, 2011); 160–181.

[147] Barack Obama, Remarks by the President on the Economy and Housing, October 24, 2011, whitehouse.gov/the-press-office/2011/10/24/remarks-president-economy-and-housing; Barack Obama, Remarks by the President on the Economy, July 25, 2013, www.whitehouse.gov/the-press-office/2013/07/25/remarks-president-economy-jacksonville-fl; Barack Obama, Remarks by the President on Opportunity for All and Skills for America's Workers, January 30, 2014, www.gpo.gov/fdsys/pks/DCPD-201400055/html/DCPD-201400055.htm

[148] Jenna Wortham, "Obama Brought Silicon Valley to Washington," *The New York Times Sunday Magazine*, October 30, 2016, MM22.

[149] Ted Johnson, "John Kerry Meets with Hollywood Studio Chiefs to Discuss ISIS," *Variety*, February 16, 2016, www.variety.com/2016/biz/news/john-kerry-hollywood-studio-chiefs-isis-1201707652/.

[150] Charles H. Franklin and Liane C. Kosaki, "Republican Schoolmaster: The U.S. Supreme Court, Public Opinion and Abortion," *American Political Science Review* 83 (1989): 751–771.

populations in need of protection. The *Casey* Court – acknowledging its public reach – called on the competing sides of the abortion debate to settle their differences, on the grounds of the Court's wisdom about what women require for freedom and identity-formation.[151] Justice Kennedy's opinions in the homosexual sex and marriage cases insisted that same-sex marriage was a result of "new insights," and "enhanced understanding" of the true needs of same-sex couples and their children, apparent in 2015 to five members of the Court.[152] Justice Sotomayor publicly touted her empathy as a "wise Latina" as a relevant qualification for a seat on the Court.[153] Justice Ginsburg has acknowledged that the Justices "dialogue" with the citizens of the United States,[154] and Justice O'Connor has spoken similarly.[155]

While it is certainly true that the public at large does not pay attention to every Supreme Court opinion, the Court's reach is undoubtedly wider where neuralgic subjects are concerned.[156] When the subject matter is sex, no matter which federal branch is involved, media attention will be widespread. This has been especially true also in recent years, when laws touching on sex have also clashed loudly with religious beliefs.

The federal stance also affects those who are touched individually by its laws and regulations. There is the real possibility, for example, that because poorer Americans interact with government bureaucracy more on matters of health care – including sex – the government's power to influence them may be greater.

The government also communicates directly with its grantees and contractors, and the clients served by each of these. Especially during the Obama administration, but also previously, executive orders and agency regulations have communicated elements of sexual expressionism to recipients of federal money.

It is also likely that, when any branch of the government speaks with "feeling" about morality or moral subjects, it wields a distinct kind of authority. This is most obvious when the subjects include civil rights or the environment. It

[151] *Casey*, 867–869.

[152] *Obergefell*, 2590, 2591.

[153] Robert Farley, "Sotomayor's comment about Latina woman versus white men," *Politifact*, May 27, 2009, www.politifact.com/truth-o-meter/statements/2009/may/27/judicial-confirmation-network/Sotomayor-comment-Latina-women-versus-white-men/.

[154] Ruth Bader Ginsburg, "Speaking in a Judicial Voice," *New York University Law Review* 67 (1998), 1198.

[155] Sandra Day O'Connor, *The Majesty of Law, Reflections of a Supreme Court Justice* (New York: Random House, 2003), 166.

[156] Franklin and Kosaki, "Republican Schoolmaster: The U.S. Supreme Court, Public Opinion and Abortion," 754.

is also likely true when the government takes up the subject of sex under the headings of civil rights, nondiscrimination, freedom or happiness, and does so using the personalistic rhetoric of identity, dignity and human equality.

Law and Culture Together

The federal voice on sexual expressionism is also undoubtedly magnified by its confluence with important cultural trends regarding sex, marriage and parenting. It could not be nearly as influential without them.

When both law and popular culture, for example, endorse a particular idea, the public might easily conclude that successful and powerful people have reached a consensus position. The overlap can also reinforce the inference that the consensus position is inevitable: that citizens are powerless to change it.

This is related to my observations above, that when the Court and the White House suggest that they are channeling public opinion effectively into law, this strengthens the influence of their ideas.

Because of these dynamics, and because the federal voice is likely to be interpreted in tandem with these trends, it is worthwhile to look briefly at some leading ideas circulating during the rise of sexual expressionism in law. A closer look reveals how they might influence, and be influenced by, the law on sexual expression. Only a lengthier book could do justice to such a collection. The following is a summary treatment only.

The Individual

The modern "turn toward the self" is a well-known phenomenon in the fields of philosophy, sociology and law, among others. It has several aspects: the notion that "finding" and becoming oneself is a source of progress; the tendency to take one's personal opinion as the only important or even the final word on a subject, possibly combined with willingness to allow other people to do likewise.[157]

Charles Taylor calls this modern phenomenon the emergence of the "buffered self:" a self which is not porous but rather disengaged from everything but its own mind. The purposes of things arise within the person. The meanings of things are the same as his or her responses to them.[158]

---

[157] Charles Taylor, *A Secular Age* (Cambridge: The Belknap Press of Harvard University, 2007), 38.
[158] Ibid.

As applied to sexual expression, this notion was explored by sociologist Pitirim A. Sorokin. In 1956 he argued that the individual was coming to "regard[ ] himself as law giver and judge entitled to juggle all moral and legal standards" about sex as he pleases.[159]

The most articulate explanation of the re-making of sex as a subjective, meaning-making enterprise is provided by Cambridge University sociologist Anthony Giddens in his landmark 1992 book, *The Transformation of Intimacy*. There, Giddens introduced the notion of "plastic sex," meaning sex with subjectively moldable meaning, unmoored from its physical structures: in particular its link with procreation. He wrote that the "decenter[ing]" of sex from reproduction began as early as the late eighteenth century, when there developed a move to limit family size, but that it became widespread with the introduction of modern contraception and assisted reproductive technologies. Once sex is severed from reproduction, he argues, it is severed from kinship, from "the generations." Its meaning is reduced to pleasure. Sexuality then becomes "a property of the individual" and "internally referential," which leads to it becoming a tool for forging self-identity, as well as a way of making connections with others not bound to any particular time. Sexuality "is now a means of forging connections with others on the basis of intimacy, no longer grounded in an immutable kinship order sustained across the generations."[160]

The *Eisenstadt* Court first redirected the law's interest in sexual expression separate from childbearing, away from the married couple and onto the individual woman, single or married, and her personal opinion ("decisions about matters so fundamentally affecting a person" ... in her "intellectual and emotional makeup"). The *Casey* Court took this one step further, suggesting that denying individual desires in connection with sexual expression and parenting was a denial of fundamental needs and rights respecting individual identity formation (defining "one's own concept" of the "universe"). The homosexual sex and marriage cases did likewise.

Another aspect of individualism involves the decline of the role of the transcendent in individual lives. Formerly, the divine was understood to be the author of all creation including the body, which was therefore a "given." One looked to the body for norms and not only for information. Today, with the decline of belief in the transcendent and the "givenness" of creation, the world, including the body, is a matter for personal interpretation. It can become more of a resource, an object of investigation, manipulation,

---

[159] Pitirim A. Sorokin, *The American Sex Revolution*, 88.
[160] Giddens, *The Transformation of Intimacy*, 2, 27, 112, 121, 144, 156, 167, 174, 175, 178–180.

improvement or even mining. The person seems "self-made." The meanings and purposes of even organic things – such as the functioning of the human body, the existence of two sexes, the link between sex and procreation – point neither to the transcendent nor to behavioral norms. The body's "givenness" is instead an obstacle, a barrier to human desires. According to this school of thought, even marriage itself, with its usual or expected structure, becomes a problem, because it has been handed down, and has a usual structure, which seems a threat to self-expression. Stigma arising out of any sexual choice likewise becomes problematic.

The federal government's declining to reason from biological facts about the human body – especially regarding the link between sex and children and the unique procreative capacities of men and women – seem closely related to this line of thought. New claims regarding sexual fluidity, and the turn to assisted reproductive technologies, are likewise related to it.

Happiness

Another cultural idea which enjoyed growing popularity in the twentieth and twenty-first centuries, concerns the centrality of sexual happiness to personal happiness and self-realization. Charles Taylor writes of the historical importance in the United States of the right to happiness generally, and points to its appearance in the Declaration of Independence. He asserts that, while this had been historically conditioned by shared ethics concerning good citizenship, self-rule, and sexual morality, these limits, especially regarding sexual mores, were set aside after World War I.[161] In Taylor's view, the modern "triumph of the therapeutic" is a closely related phenomenon. Traditional ideas about morality are subordinated to the imperative of personal fulfillment, and becoming our "authentic selves."[162]

Margaret Sanger picked up the theme of sexual freedom as happiness, in the context of arguments about birth control. She predicted that sex unlinked with children (by means of contraception) would make a husband for his wife "a veritable god – worthy of her profoundest worship.... Through sex mankind may attain the great spiritual illumination which will transform the world, which will light up the holy path to an earthly paradise."[163] Later feminists – Betty Friedan in her *Feminine Mystique* and Simone de Beauvoir in

---

[161] Taylor, *A Secular Age*, 485–493.
[162] *Id.* at 618–620, 507–508.
[163] Margaret Sanger, *Happiness in Marriage* (Garden City: Blue Ribbon Books, 1940), 121, 126, 271.

The Second Sex – also predicted significant, positive transformations of male/ female relations if sex could be separated from children.[164]

Historian Steven Seidman writes that a sense began to emerge in the early twentieth century that sexual unhappiness bore an important share of the blame for weakening marriages. Couples needed better sexual experiences and also to recognize that women had sexual needs. He further chronicles the rise of the notion that, even apart from a romantic context, good sex is important to the free and self-actualized human being because of its association with the values of choice, variety, intimacy, pleasure and the ability to manifest identities previously hidden.[165]

The right to happiness was applied to the sexual context by the man who invented the term "the sexual revolution." In his book *Die Sexuelle Revolution*, famous Freudian disciple Wilhelm Reich wrote that the "core of life's happiness is sexual happiness."[166] This theme is sounded especially in the homosexual sex and marriage cases. It is in *Lawrence's* insistence that one's very identity is coextensive with one's sexual acts, and in *Obergefell's* definition of marriage as sex plus commitment, which could answer human being's "universal fear that a lonely person might call out only to find no one there. It offers the hope of companionship and understanding and assurance that while both still live there will be someone to care for the other."[167]

Sex as Revolutionary

Another idea that gained power from the mid-twentieth century is the notion that sexual license is itself a tool for overthrowing traditional and repressive authority. This is most directly channeled by the Supreme Court, and in other federal statements about the personal and social freedom gained by women and LGBT persons, in connection with contraception or abortion or same-sex marriage. A surprising number and diversity of thinkers have explored it.

Hebrew University sociologist Eva Illouz speculates that the idea of socially forbidden sexual expression originated with popular stories about taboo or star-crossed love. In these stories love is irruptive, and has the potential to

---

[164] Betty Friedan, *The Feminine Mystique* (New York: W.W. Norton and Co., Inc. 1963), 86; Simone de Beauvoir, *The Second Sex*, ed. and trans. H. M. Parshley (New York: Vintage Books (Reprint), 1989), 724–731.

[165] Seidman, *Romantic Longings*, 4, 5, 83, 85, 123,193–194, 202.

[166] Wilhelm Reich, *The Sexual Revolution: Toward a Self-Regulating Character Structure*, trans. Therese Pol (New York: Farrar, Straus and Giroux, 1945), 88.

[167] *Obergefell*, 2600.

undermine authority and cross social lines. As such, it could potentially possess transcendent or sacred (though nonreligious) properties.[168]

Early twentieth century journalist and social critic Walter Lippman noted the tendency in the 1920s to associate overthrowing traditional sexual mores with women's empowerment.[169] Philosopher Charles Taylor describes the emergence of the wider belief that persons formerly cast out of polite society on the grounds of their sexual conduct – or anyone repressed by bourgeois conventions – could be liberated by transgressive sex, because it brought the person in touch with, and linked, mind and body, reason and feeling. It was a reaction against old taboos and the double standard. There emerged the idea that it might even create a brotherhood of men.[170] Taylor notes, however, how such a movement succumbed to utopianism, and neglected the dilemmas and moral hazards which beset sexual relations, as well as the significant potential that new sexual mores would immiserate women by transforming them into objects for men.[171]

American literature professor Robert Oscar Lopez also identifies historical signs of the belief that transgressive sex is revolutionary. He highlights pornography, the use of women's bodies in advertising, and literature such as *The Crucible*, which "reinforced the association in Americans' minds between sexually judgmental Puritans and their penchant for political persecution."[172]

Youth Culture

Also on the rise, coincident with the rise of sexual expressionism in law, was "youth culture." As described by Irish social critic John Waters,[173] youth culture communicates that the ideal human state and the meaning of life is youth, including rebellion against conventions. American media critic Neil Postman[174] proposes how youth culture unfolded in the United States. He claims that the second half of the twentieth century scrambled the norms

---

[168] Eva Illouz, *Consuming the Romantic Utopia: Love and the Cultural Contradictions of Capitalism* (Berkley: The University of California Press, 1997), 8.

[169] Walter Lippmann, *A Preface to Morals* (New York: The Macmillan Company, 1929), 290–307.

[170] Taylor, *A Secular Age*, 616.

[171] Taylor, *A Secular Age*, 616, 502.

[172] Robert Oscar Lopez, "Civil Rights and the Sexual Revolution Need a Divorce," *The Federalist*, April 19, 2016, at www.thefederalist.com/2016/04/19/civil-rights-and-the-sexual-revolution-need-a-divorce/.

[173] John Waters, *Beyond Consolation: How We Became too "Clever" for God and Our Own Good* (London: Bloomsbury Academic, 2010), 40–41.

[174] Neil Postman, *The Disappearance of Childhood* (New York: Vintage Books, 1994), 99, 127–137.

applicable to adults' and children's behavior. He charges the media with redu-cing itself to childish levels, by using more pictures and less rational argu-ment. He also claims that adults sought out less responsibility and childish things for themselves, like children's play, television habits, and the demand for instant gratification. Children, meanwhile, were permitted access to adult things such as exposure to sex, which was removed from the category of pro-found adult mystery and became a product for all.

The federal government's focus on sexual expression as freedom, its exten-sion of contraception and abortion rights to minors, and its explicit pride in overthrowing notions of marriage and sex which are tied to children, find an echo in both of these trends. Adults as youth aren't required to be parental. Youth as adults can be imagined to be resilient or independent, and thus not in need of adult protection.

A Reduced Valuation of Children

Beginning especially in the 1960s, fears of a "population bomb" began to cast a shadow on the value of children. At the same time, with the rise of a femin-ist consciousness, children were increasingly seen as hindrances to women's growing education and employment opportunities. By this time too, due to the decline of the family farm and child labor, children were also rarely con-tributing to a household's income. They were consumers not producers.

Federal birth control programs responded to each of these themes regard-ing children. They spoke about reducing the numbers of children, especially among the poor. They spoke in terms of empowering women. The abortion cases, too, characterized unwanted children as tremendous burdens and notably failed to speak about the positive aspects of childbearing. Likewise, *Obergefell* held that a state could not identify anything of special value in a married couple's ability to procreate children.

Technology

There is a very powerful American notion that what is stated or offered as "sci-ence" is objectively true and in a sense socially "inevitable" if progress is to be achieved. This is sometimes referred to as the "technological imperative." Philosopher Hans Jonas – widely credited for developing the most powerful ethical theory regarding responsibility for the environment and for technol-ogy – wrote at length regarding how to turn the technological imperative on its head. His book *The Imperative of Responsibility: In Search of an Ethics for the Technological Age*,[175] was intended to help human beings break free of the notion that an "ought" follows a scientific claim of an "is."

The general enthusiasm with which the pill and later contraceptives were accepted and linked to women's freedom, is linked to the "technological imperative." Deference to science may also go a long way toward explaining continued federal dedication to a contraception solution to the problem of disadvantaged children, despite contraceptives' current failure to ameliorate rates of nonmarital and unintended births.

Sex and Materialism

More than a few scholars have explored the twentieth century predilection to conceive of sex and its positive effects as a consumer item. Generally, they propose that the norm of capitalist materialism – of consuming as pleasure and self-expression and self-fulfillment – has invaded the sexual arena. Professor Illouz points out that this idea overlaps with the idea of transgressive sex as freedom, and affirms a "consumerist idiom of postmodern culture ... promising transgression through the consuming of leisure and Nature."[176] She reports on research revealing contemporary individuals' strong tendencies to associate romance with the consumption of expensive things and exotic places.

Journalist Peggy Orenstein illustrated the phenomenon by means of interviews with female college students. One student reported trying to "perform" sex for the pleasure of her partner, like the porn stars she knows men watch. She recounted: "[i]f the position is really hard, I think about I can do it, like watching myself, like a porn star."[177]

Philosopher Cynthia Willett observes how "[n]either the intimate pleasures of private sexual fantasy nor the quiet reflections of the intellectual operate in a space devoid of the images, rhythms, and techno-curves of consumer culture or corporate-sponsored infotainment."[178] These are rather omnipresent, and whether employed as advertising or entertainment, treat sex as a consumption good, and use sex to sell consumer products.[179]

[175] Hans Jonas, *The Imperative of Responsibility: In Search of an Ethics for the Technological Age* (Chicago: The University of Chicago Press, 1984).
[176] Illouz, *Consuming the Romantic Utopia: Love and the Cultural Contradictions of Capitalism*, 8–10.
[177] Peggy Orenstein, *Girls and Sex: Navigating the Complicated New Landscape* (New York: Harper, 2016), 37–38.
[178] Cynthia Willett, *The Soul of Justice* (Ithaca: Cornell University Press, 2001), 6.
[179] Seidman, *Romantic Longings*, 123–124.

A great deal of federal material – including *Casey*, *Lawrence*, the same-sex marriage cases, and executive agencies' sexual advice materials – demonstrates a tendency to view spontaneous sex and marriage recognition as valuable consumption goods.

Casey refers to women's ability to secure better lives through access to "unplanned activity" insured against childbearing. *Lawrence* and *Obergefell* speak of the identity affirmation, and of the social and financial benefits people obtain by means of sex or marriage.

CONCLUSION

The federal government's approach to sexual expression ranges from insufficiently attentive to recklessly indifferent toward children's wellbeing, especially as it is tied to their family structure. The government wields a great deal of power, alone and in tandem with cultural and philosophical notions which also tend to valorize the individual and sexual happiness.

This would be a surprising situation at any time, considering children's needs, but it particularly surprising today in the presence of so much research about what children need to thrive. The next chapter briefly summarizes current research on the relationship between nonmarital parenting and children's welfare.

2

Nonmarital Birth and Child Outcomes

This book is primarily a description and critique of the federal government's sexual expressionist stance and its legal and policy responses. I claim that it is irresponsible or worse for the government to remain indifferent or inadequately proactive regarding nonmarital birth, especially in light of what society owes children. For reasons of length, the book cannot also be a review of the extraordinary amount of sociological, psychological and economic literature about family structure effects and children's outcomes. Regarding this enormous body of literature, I will only establish that there are sound reasons to believe that children conceived nonmaritally experience disadvantages which stem at least in part from the common challenges that follow from being born to unmarried parents.

Furthermore, there already exist numerous and well-executed books, public and private reports, and peer-reviewed articles parsing the relevant data. Many of these are cited in the notes accompanying this section. Among the most helpful books are Sara McLanahan and Gary Sandefur's classic *Growing Up With a Single Parent: What Helps, What Hurts*,[1] W. Bradford Wilcox and Nicholas Wolfinger's *Soulmates: Religion, Sex, Love, and Marriage Among African Americans and Latinos*,[2] Charles Murray's *Coming Apart: The State of White America, 1960–2010*,[3] June Carbone and Naomi Cahn's *Marriage Markets: How Inequality is Remaking the American Family*,[4] Kay Hymowitz's

---

[1]   Sara McLanahan and Gary Sandefur, *Growing Up with a Single Parent: What Hurts, What Helps* (Cambridge: Harvard University Press, 1997).

[2]   W. Bradford Wilcox and Nicholas H. Wolfinger, *Soul Mates: Religion, Sex, Love, and Marriage among African Americans and Latinos* (New York: Oxford University Press, 2016).

[3]   Charles Murray, *Coming Apart: The State of White America, 1960–2010* (New York: Crown Forum, 2012).

[4]   June Carbone and Naomi Cahn, *Marriage Markets: How Inequality is Remaking the American Family* (Oxford: Oxford University Press, 2014).

Marriage and Caste in America: Separate and Unequal Families in a Post-Marital Age,[5] and Kathryn Edin and Maria Kefalas' heartbreaking and beautiful *Promises I Can Keep: Why Poor Women Put Motherhood Before Marriage.*[6]

From these sources one can glean the following salient conclusions, which together are sufficient to dispute the verity and the ethics of a sexual expressionist posture.

First, there is a consensus that nonmarital birth itself often (though not always) yields in its wake a variety of outcomes for children in various domains including the cognitive, educational, emotional and economic.

Second, the pathways or mediators of these negative influences are many. They include many things that are more apt to happen when a mother and father are not married and may include: the absence of the second parent's income, and time for supervision, guidance and interaction; lower investments in the child because the father is an absent or cohabiting parent; loss of the second parent's personal and social capital, discipline and protection; loss of the parents' mutual support for one another and for one another's parenting; less extended family support; and household instability, due to the greater likelihood that an unmarried parent will re-partner after the child's birth, or even have additional children by a different partner.[7] Multi-partner fertility complicates parents' and children's emotional and residential stability even further, and commonly reduces the biological fathers' investments into their children.[8] Furthermore, nonmarital childbearing may yield worse outcomes for children than living in post-divorce households; research regularly indicates that fathers who never married have more modest involvement in the lives of their children.[9]

Empirical literature is particularly helpful in fleshing out several of the above conclusions about these mediating factors. It shows the following: attending to children's brain development, beginning even prenatally and continuing

5 Kay Hymowitz, *Marriage and Caste in America: Separate and Unequal Families in a Post-Marital Age* (Chicago: Ivan R. Dee, 2006).

6 Kathryn Edin and Maria J. Kefalas, *Promises I Can Keep: Why Poor Women Put Motherhood Before Marriage* (Berkeley: University of California Press, 2011).

7 McLanahan and Sandefur, *Growing Up with a Single Parent*, 1–4; Sara McLanahan, Laura Tach, and Daniel Schneider, "The Causal Effects of Father Absence," *Annual Review of Sociology* 39 (2013): 399–427.

8 Karen Benjamin Guzzo, "New Partners, More Kids: Multiple-Partner Fertility in the United States," *Annals of the American Academy of Political and Social Science* 654 (2014): 66–86.

9 Paul Amato et al., "Changes in Nonresident Father-Child Contact from 1976 to 2002," *Family Relations* 58 (2009), 41; William Marsiglio et al., "Scholarship on Fatherhood in the 1990s and Beyond," *Journal of Marriage and Family* 62 (2000), 1184.

especially during the first several years of the child's life, is crucial.[10] This is one of the most widely recognized recent findings in child development literature, here and abroad, by both public and private institutions and research organizations.

Even prenatally, children whose mothers lack a supportive partner can suffer from higher levels of stress, which can affect the child's health and even brain architecture.[11] After birth, children's minds develop in response to a great deal of warm and responsive verbal interaction, including open-ended questions and symbolic references. The loss of a second parent, or a family environment permitting a generous amount of time for these types of interactions, can have long-term negative consequences for children's development.[12] Nobel prize-winning economist James Heckman summarized "decades" of research in economics, neuroscience and developmental psychology to conclude that: "[l]ater attainments [of skills] build on foundations that are laid down early;" "[e]arly family environments are major predictors of cognitive and noncognitive abilities;" "[d]isadvantage is associated with poor parenting practices and lack of positive cognitive and noncognitive stimulation;" and "[a] child who falls behind may never catch up."[13]

On average, even two biological, cohabiting parents do not deliver the degree of investment in their children that marital parenting delivers, due in large part to selection effects, couple instability, habits and expectations.[14]

Among other factors, mothers' parenting is influenced by partner support, and fathers' parenting is influenced by his attachment to the mother. In other words, while each parent very likely offers a unique contribution to their child,[15] there are also contributions that emerge as a result of partnership synergies and dynamics.[16]

[10] Roger Thurow, *The First 1000 Days: A Crucial Time for Mothers and Children – and the World* (Philadelphia: Public Affairs, 2016), 78.

[11] First 1001 Days All Party Parliamentary Group, *Building Great Britons: Conception to Age Two*, www.1001criticaldays.co.uk.

[12] Betty Hart and Todd R. Risley, *Meaningful Differences in the Everyday Experience of Young American Children* (Baltimore: Paul H. Brookes Publishing Co., 1995).

[13] James C. Heckman, "Skill Formation and the Economics of Investing in Disadvantaged Children," *Science* 312 (2006), 1900–1901.

[14] Wendy D. Manning, "Cohabitation and Child Wellbeing," *The Future of Children* 25 (2015), 51–61; Scott Stanley, "Positive Child Outcomes: Commitment, Signaling, and Sequence," Institute for Family Studies, September 18, 2014, www.family-studies.org/marriage-and-positive-child-outcomes-commitment-signaling-and-sequence/.

[15] Michael Yogman and Craig F. Garfield, "Father's Roles in the Care and Development of their Children," *Pediatrics* 138, no. 1 (2016), doi: 10.1542/peds.2016-1128; see US Department of Health and Human Services, "Responsible Fatherhood: New Pathways for Fathers and Families Demonstration Grants," Office of Family Assistance (2016), www.acf.hhs.gov/ofa/programs/healthy-marriage/responsible-fatherhood.

[16] David Ribar, "Why Marriage Matters for Child Wellbeing," *The Future of Children* 25, no. 2 (2015), 11–23; US Department of Health and Human Services, *"The Importance of Fathers in*

Instability appears to be one of the most important mediators of nonmarital children's disadvantage.[17] That is, it is the pathway by which the disadvantage may happen. An emerging literature documents the unstable trajectories of most nonmarital households, especially as compared to marital households. In the words of one sociologist "[f]amily structure at birth sets the stage for subsequent instability."[18] Mothers are unlikely to later marry the child's father and even if they do, their divorce rates are high. Cohabiting nonmarital partnerships are even less stable. Low percentages of children are likely to be with their biological mother and father, even by age three.[19] The later introduction of an unrelated male into a household is, on average, disruptive or worse for children.[20]

The third salient conclusion, regarding the relationship between nonmarital parenting and child outcomes, is that causation runs in both directions. Poverty, fewer years of education, unstable neighborhoods, family structure deficits, reduced employment prospects, and a history involving crime or drugs, predict for higher rates of nonmarital parenting.[21] As described immediately above, however, the temporal, financial, personal, and social realities of nonmarital parenting help to cause poorer outcomes for children born into these circumstances.

the *Healthy Development of Children*," by Jeffrey Rosenberg and W. Bradford Wilcox, US Department of Health and Human Services (Washington, D.C., 2006), www.childwelfare. gov/pubPDFs/fatherhood.pdf; Paul R. Amato, "More than Money? Men's Contributions to Their Children's Lives," in *Men in Families: When Do they Get Involved? What Difference Does It Make?* ed. Alan Booth and Ann C. Crouter (New York: Psychology Press, 1998), 241–278.

[17] Dohoon Lee and Sara McLanahan, "Family Structure Transitions and Child Development: Instability, Selection, and Population Heterogeneity," *American Sociological Review* 80, no. 4 (2015): 738–63; ed. Gary W. Evans and Theodore D. Wachs, *Chaos and Its Influence on Children's Development: An Ecological Perspective* (Washington, D.C.: American Psychological Association, 2009).

[18] Manning, "Cohabitation and Child Wellbeing," 57–58.

[19] Sara McLanahan, "Diverging Destinies: How Children are Faring under the Second Demographic Transition," *Demography* 41, no. 4 (2004), 607.

[20] Martin Daly and Margo Wilson, "The 'Cinderella effect': Elevated Mistreatment of Stepchildren in Comparison to Those Living with Genetic Parents," www.cep.ucsb.edu/ buller/cinderella%20effect%20facts.pdf; US Department of Justice, *Violence against Women: A National Crime Victimization Survey Report*, by Ronet Bachman, U.S. Department of Justice (Washington, D.C., 1994), www.ncjrs.gov/pdffiles1/Digitization/145325NCJRS.pdf; W. Bradford Wilcox, "#YesWomenAndChildren Are Safer Within Intact Marriages," *The Federalist*, January 6, 2015, www.thefederalist.com/2015/01/06/yesallwomenandchildren-are-safer-within-intact-marriages/.

[21] US Department of Health and Human Services, "*Family Structure and Nonmarital Fertility: Perspectives from Ethnographic Research*," by Linda M. Burton, US Department of Health and Human Services (Hyattsville, MD, 1995), 147–165.

Fourth, scholarly and political leaders across the ideological continuum increasingly share the opinion that causation runs in both directions. More often, in recent years, they are joining together to propose that public and private efforts aim both to promote marital childbearing directly, and to address the many factors that lead to it.[22] This is a very promising sign, and an important part of my decision to author this book. There are many well-developed and encouraging ideas to provide more generous and better-designed programs and services to facilitate marriage and marital childbearing; but there are, as yet, insufficient concrete initiatives directly promoting marital childbearing.

Fifth, lower income is an important factor respecting both the causes and the consequences of nonmarital parenting. An adult with fewer financial resources is more likely to have been raised with a single-parent, have fewer likely marriage partners in her community, and is more likely to perceive lower "opportunity costs" of a nonmarital pregnancy – that is, she perceives a reduced set of opportunities for higher education or promising employment.[23]

At the same time, the loss of a second parent's financial contribution importantly affects a child's life chances – for example, respecting better healthcare, educational, and residential opportunities. Thus, even while it is regularly concluded that nonmarital parenting exerts negative influences upon child outcomes even *after* controlling for income, it is important to remember that lower income is also a factor which nests closely with the loss of a second parent.[24] According to the nonpartisan research institution Child Trends, income differences only partly account for the numerous difficulties of living without a married, two-parent family.[25] Family Scholar Isabel Sawhill adds that the social mobility of even the poorest children is boosted in part due to the greater income of two stable parents.[26]

---

[22] Emily Badger, "The Terrible Loneliness of Growing Up Poor in Robert Putnam's America," *The Washington Post*, March 6, 2015, www.washingtonpost.com/news/wonk/wp/2015/03/06/the-terrible-loneliness-of-growing-up-poor-in-robert-putnams-america/?utm_term=.6f3ebfc854a3; Brookings Institution and American Enterprise Institute, *Opportunity, Responsibility and Security: A Consensus Plan for Reducing Poverty and Restoring the American Dream* www.brookings.edu/wp-content/uploads/2016/07/Full-Report.pdf.

[23] Sara McLanahan and Christine Percheski, "Family Structure and the Reproduction of Inequalities," *Annual Review of Sociology* 34 (2008): 257–276.

[24] Susan E. Mayer, *What Money Can't Buy: Family Income and Children's Life Chances* (Cambridge: Harvard University Press, 1998), 155.

[25] Child Trends, "Family Structure: Indicators on Children and Youth," www.childtrends.org/wp-content/uploads/2015/03/59_Family_Structure.pdf.

[26] Nathan Pippenger, "Arguments Q + A: Isabel Sawhill, Author of *Generation Unbound*," *Democracy: A Journal of Ideas*, October 17, 2014, www.democracyjournal.org/arguments/arguments-qa-isabel-sawhill-author-of-generation-unbound/.

Sixth, selection effects are not a complete explanation for the difficulties faced by nonmarital children. "Selection effects" refers to the notion that there are characteristics that lead some partners to have marital children, and thereafter provide them with certain advantages, as distinguished from the characteristics that lead others to have nonmarital children, thereby disadvantaging those children.

Selection effects undoubtedly play a role in the diminished outcomes of nonmarital children, but they are not the whole story. Professor McLanahan, for example, highlights important attributes of marriage which are not tied to the adults' prior tastes or gifts, but which nevertheless profoundly influence children: parenting time and guidance, individual human capital and community ties, resources available from extended family and friends, and a reduction of stress for each parent due to the presence of the other.[27] Sociologist W. Bradford Wilcox and economist Robert Lerman also point to the effects of marriage itself upon men. To wit: married men work more hours and adopt more stable employment habits than single men of comparable backgrounds, races, educations, and ethnicity – quite possibly due to the influence of being married and a parent.[28]

Looking at proposed "genetic selection effects," researchers today appear to believe that children's outcomes could not be tied strictly to parental traits or genes. They hold, rather, that the interactions between a child's genes and all of that child's various environments, together sculpt brain development. James Heckman explains that the "architecture of the brain and the process of skill formation are influenced by an interaction between genetics and individual experience."[29] This explanation leaves a great deal of room for children's environments to play an important role in their development.

Seventh, and finally, more and more scholars are documenting the close relationship between nonmarital births and a variety of disturbing social gaps.[30] There are both widening and hardening gaps – in levels of wealth and

---

[27] Sara McLanahan, "Fragile Families and the Reproduction of Poverty," *Annals of the American Academy of Political and Social Science*, 621, no. 1 (2009): 111–131.

[28] Robert I. Lerman and W. Bradford Wilcox, *For Richer, For Poorer: How Family Structures Economic Success in America* (Washington, D.C.: American Enterprise Institute and Institute for Family Studies, 2014), 33–35.

[29] Heckman, "Skill Formation and the Economics of Investing in Disadvantaged Children," 1900.

[30] McLanahan, "Diverging Destinies: How Children are Faring under the Second Demographic Transition;" Thomas Piketty, Steven Durlauf and Kevin Murphy, "Three Views on Inequality," *The University of Chicago Magazine*, (2016), 22–25; McLanahan "Family Structure and the Reproduction of Inequalities;" W. Bradford Wilcox, "The Evolution of Divorce," *National Affairs* 81 (2009); Hymowitz, *Marriage and Caste in America; Ralph Richard Banks, Is Marriage For White People? How the African American Marriage Decline Affects Everyone* (New York: Penguin, 2011).

income, and in marriage, education, and employment prospects – between high and low socioeconomic classes, white and black Americans, and even between females and males who were both reared by a single-mother. One 2014 study[31] even concluded that the strongest and most robust predictor of economic mobility at the community level is the fraction of children living with single parents. It showed that children who are raised in communities with high percentages of single parents are far less likely to move into a higher socioeconomic stratum as adults. The author, Harvard economist Raj Chetty, is careful to note that his study does not indicate causation, and that the many other factors predicting mobility – racial and economic segregation, school quality, and others – are mutually intertwined with family structure. Still, given the amount of scholarship documenting that family structure is both the cause and the consequence of economic and social disadvantages, this study reveals the important attention that nonmarital parenting merits in connection with improving social mobility.

Regarding racial and socioeconomic gaps between individuals, economists and sociologists measure these in many ways. Their conclusions, however, are similar. White and higher-income Americans – who are also more likely to have completed more years of education – are more likely to marry and have children within marriage. Black and lower-income Americans – who are also less likely to have a college education – are less likely to marry and more likely to have children apart from marriage.[32] These gaps are then formed and reinforced by the tendency for nonmarital parenting to persist intergnerationally,[33] and the tendency for advantaged individuals to "consolidate" their advantages – and pass them on to their children – by marrying

---

[31]   Raj Chetty et al., "Where is the Land of Opportunity? The Geography of Intergenerational Mobility in the United States," *The Quarterly Journal of Economics* 129, no. 4 (2014): 1553–1623.

[32]   Rakesh Kochhar and Richard Fry, "Wealth Inequality Has Widened Along Racial, Ethnic Lines Since the End of the Great Recession," Pew Research Fact Tank, December 19, 2014, www.pewresearch.org/fact-tank/2014/12/12/racial-wealth-gaps-great-recession/; General Social Survey, 1972–2021, Trends in Marriage, Adults Aged 20–54, by Race/Ethnicity; National Center for Health Statistics, *Births: Preliminary Data for 2006*," by B.E. Hamilton, J.A. Martin and S.J. Ventura, National Center for Health Statistics (Hyattsville, MD, 2007), www.cdc.gov/nchs/data/nvsr/nvsr56/nvsr56_07.pdf; National Center for Health Statistics, *Births: Preliminary Data for 2012*, by B.E. Hamilton, J.A. Martin and S. J. Ventura, National Center for Health Statistics (Hyattsville, MD, 2012); US Census Bureau, *Current Population Surveys, March Demographic Supplement, 1970–2013.*

[33]   McLanahan, "Fragile Families and the Reproduction of Poverty," 111–131; Robin S. Högnäs and Marcia J. Carlson, "Like Parent, Like Child? The Intergenerational Transmission of Nonmarital Childbearing," *Social Science Research* 41, no. 6 (2012): 1480–1494.

others similar to themselves. This latter phenomenon is called "assortative mating."[34]

Because black Americans have a longer history of high nonmarital birth-rates, lower incomes, and fewer years of education – due to many factors including a long legacy of slavery and racial discrimination – the race gap, as well as the income and wealth gaps, are mutually reinforcing in a negative direction.

Regarding males and females, recent research documents that boys reared without their fathers are more likely to underperform economically and educationally over the long run, when compared to their sisters.[35] Researchers are suggesting the influence of various factors: boys' potential greater sensitivity to lower parental inputs (attention and warmth); the possibility that girls see their single mothers as successful role models for themselves, while boys lack a same-sex role model; or mothers' devoting more time to daughters than sons.

In sum, there is more than enough evidence to conclude that it is unwise, even unethical, for the federal government to speak to adults in a sexual expressionist voice respecting nonmarital birth. When adults act in a sexual expressionist fashion, not only do large numbers of individual children suffer from the effects of their family structure, but also the American ideals of fairness, opportunity, and mobility are seriously compromised. Chapter Three sets out the two leading federal responses to the disadvantages experienced by children born apart from marriage.

---

[34] Robert D. Mare, "Educational Homogamy in Two Gilded Ages: Evidence from Intergenerational Social Mobility Data," *Annals of the American Academy of Political and Social Science* 663, no. 1 (2016): 117–139.

[35] Claire Cain Miller, "A Disadvantaged Start Hurts Boys More than Girls," *New York Times*, October 22, 2015, www.nytimes.com/2015/10/22/upshot/a-disadvantaged-start-hurts-boys-more-than-girls.html; David Autor et al., "Family Disadvantage and the Gender Gap in Behavioral and Educational Outcomes" (working paper, Institute for Policy Research, Northwestern University, 2015), www.ipr.northwestern.edu/publications/docs/workingpapers/2015/IPR-WP-15–16.pdf; Marianne Bertrand and Jessica Pan, "The Trouble with Boys: Social Influences and the Gender Gap in Disruptive Behavior," *American Economic Journal of Applied Economics* 5, no. 1 (2013): 1–35.

3

To Treat the Wounded or to Prevent their Birth

Two Federal Responses

This chapter will examine the two leading federal responses to the difficulties regularly facing nonmarital children and their families: social welfare benefits and programs, and contraception. Obviously, social welfare benefits are directed more broadly to solving problems – including, for example, poverty, parenting time deficits, father absence – which might occur in a variety of households, not just nonmarital households. They benefit a particularly large number of single-parent and poor households. Because fifty percent of single-parent homes are nonmarital homes, it is safe to say that federal social welfare programs and benefits are, for all practical purposes, an important response to the phenomenon of nonmarital birth.

Federal social welfare programs can be characterized broadly as "back door" efforts – referring again to Professor Browning's language – given that they assist children only after their parents have made the choices which determine a child's family formation at the front door.

A second federal response to nonmarital parenting is contraception, which, according to common and contemporary federal usage, also includes some drugs and devices that are not truly "contraceptive," but may act post-fertilization, according to the Food and Drug Administration.[1] Today, this second category is increasingly dominated by federal efforts to promote the use of LARCs such as intrauterine devices (IUDs), implants and injections.

BACK DOOR

Federal efforts to assist poor children are vast. The Urban Institute estimates that the federal government annually spends over 471 billion dollars on

---

[1] Kelly Wallace, "Health and Human Services Kathleen Sebelius Tells iVillage 'Historic' New Guidelines Cover Contraception, Not Abortion," *iVillage*, August 2, 2011, www.pages.citebite.com/n1r2c8f2s7bhb (accessed January 30, 2017).

children.[2] A great deal of this spending finds its way into single-parent homes, given that they are far more likely to suffer poverty. According the US Census Bureau, the poverty rate for all families is about twelve percent. For children living in single-mother homes – eighty-four percent of all single-parenting households[3] – the poverty rate is thirty-one percent. By comparison, for married families the rate is about six percent.[4]

There are too many federal programs and benefits even to list, let alone to fully describe in the space of this book. I will therefore confine myself to those most likely directed to the circumstances obtaining in nonmarital homes. Before turning to a more detailed description of these, allow me to offer two introductory observations. First, while all of the programs below are federal, some also partner with states, which expend their own, additional resources. Sometimes federal agencies contract with or supply grants to private organizations, too, in order to carry out a federal plan.

Second, the variety and the cost of these programs testify not only to Americans' good will toward children and families in need, but also to the size and variety of losses experienced by many nonmarital families. By its involvement, and by the contents of its programs, the federal government acknowledges these. Of course, nonmarital families' situations are influenced by many factors I note regularly in this volume; but the loss of the second, married parent is an important one.

Income

I turn first to the set of programs addressing families' most basic needs. Temporary Assistance to Needy Families ("TANF"), popularly known as "welfare," provides income to poor families. It began in 1935 as Aid to Families with Dependent Children, providing cash assistance to poor families with children. In 1996, it was renamed TANF in the Personal Responsibility and Work Opportunity Reconciliation Act (popularly known as welfare reform).

The federal government issues TANF grants to states, which then distribute cash assistance to citizens who meet financial criteria established by the state. Amounts vary according to family size, and recipients must abide by

---

[2] Sara Edelstein, *The Urban Institute, Kids' Share 2016: Federal Expenditures on Children Through 2015 and Future Projections* (Washington, DC: The Urban Institute, 2016).

[3] US Census Bureau, *Families and Living Arrangements 2014*, Table FG6, One-Parent Unmarried Family Groups with Own Children/1 Under 18, by Marital Status of the Reference Person: 2014.

[4] US Census Bureau, *Income and Poverty in the United States*, Bernadette D. Proctor, et al., US Census Bureau, Report No. P60-256 (September 13, 2014), Table 4. Families in Poverty by Type of Family.

the rules established by the state. Some states, for example, require mothers to provide paternity information and may require certain work-related activities. States must also expend a certain level of funds, called the Maintenance of Effort ("MOE") requirement. In 2014, states distributed nearly thirty-two billion dollars in combined federal TANF and state MOE funds; 16.5 billion dollars represented the federal contribution (a figure that has not changed since 1996).[5]

An individual's TANF eligibility is ordinarily limited to sixty months, though hardship exceptions are possible. States may and do spend TANF and MOE dollars for a variety of purposes: care for children in their own homes; preparation for work, employment or marriage; out-of-wedlock pregnancy prevention or reduction; and encouraging the formation of two-parent families. States vary widely in their allocation of dollars as between these purposes. According to the Center for Budget and Policy Priorities,[6] in 2014, states spent only twenty-six percent of their Federal and State TANF dollars providing income assistance to recipients. Thirty-four percent was directed to "other areas" including pregnancy prevention and two-parent family formation, juvenile justice, foster care and child welfare, parenting training, substance abuse treatment, domestic violence services, early education, teen pregnancy prevention, visiting nurse services, and-after school programs. On average, of this thirty-four percent, about one percent was directed at two-parent family formation and maintenance.

Federal data summarizing the characteristics of TANF recipients in 2012 reported that "[t]he average number of persons in TANF families was 2.4, including an average of 1.8 recipient children." In other words, the average household has less than one parent. It further reported that "[i]n twenty-three states, the District of Columbia and two territories, there were no two-parent family cases aided with Federal TANF funds. . . ." Women were over eighty-five percent of adult recipients.[7]

Unlike TANF, which can benefit families with no earned income, the Earned Income Tax Credit ("EITC") distributes a cash lump sum at tax-return time, calculated on the basis of income, marital status and the number

---

[5]   Liz Schott et al., "How States Use Federal and State Funds Under the TANF Block Grant," The Center for Budget and Policy Priorities, October 15, 2015, www.cbpp.org/research/family-income-support/how-states-use-federal-and-state-funds-under-the-tanf-block-grant.

[6]   Ibid.

[7]   US Department of Health and Human Services, *Characteristics and Financial Circumstances of TANF Recipients, Fiscal Year 2010* (August 8, 2012), at www.acf.hhs.gov/ofa/resource/character/fy2010/fy2010-chap10-ys-final.

of dependent children.[8] Over two dozen states have their own EITC in addition to the federal one. Some states use portions of their TANF funds to maintain a state EITC. The value of the EITC grows with additional earnings until reaching a maximum value, thus creating an incentive to work. Over twenty-six million families received an EITC in 2015. For 2016, a single parent with two children and 20,000 dollars in income would receive over 5,000 dollars, or the equivalent of about 425 dollars per month, as a result of the federal EITC. The federal government spent about six billion dollars in fiscal year 2010 on the EITC.[9] Single filers with children account for almost sixty percent of EITC filers and about three-quarters of the total cost of the program.[10] The EITC is a family policy that both conservative and liberal advocates tend to support.

Child Support

Child support is an important source of income for single parents. Federal data indicates that the child support it helps to collect provides a large percentage – forty-one percent – of receiving families' income. The federal government spends considerable resources on child support collection. The federal Child Support Enforcement Program[11] assists families who receive TANF and families who do not. It was created by Congress in 1975 to reduce net public spending on welfare by increasing private noncustodial parents' contributions. All 50 states have CSE programs and receive federal matching funds. The CSE program provides services on behalf of child support collection including, *inter alia*: parent locator services, paternity establishment, enforcement and modification of child support orders, and collection and distribution of child support. Federal law also requires states to enact the Uniform Interstate Family Support Act in order to facilitate interstate establishment, collection, modification and enforcement of child support orders.

[8]   Center for Budget and Policy Priorities, *Policy Basics: The Earned Income Tax Credit*, October 21, 2016 at www.cbpp.org/research/federal-tax/policy-basics-the-earned-income-tax-credit.

[9]   The Center for Budget and Policy Priorities, Policy Basics: the Earned Income Tax Credit, October 21, 2016, www.cbpp.org/research/federal-tax/policy-basics-the-earned-income-tax-credit.

[10] Hilary W. Hoynes and Ankur J. Patel, "Effective Policy for Reducing Inequality? The Earned Income Tax Credit and the Distribution of Income" (NBER Working Paper No. 21340, July 2015), http:www.nber.org/papers/w21340.

[11] Carmen Solomon-Fears, *Analysis of Federal-State Financing of the Child Support Enforcement Program*, Congressional Research Service (Report RL 33422, July 19, 2012), www.greenbook. waysandmeans.house.gov/sites/greenbook.waysandmeans.house.gov/files/2012/documents/ RL33422_gb.pdf.

Federal law further facilitates international child support enforcement, and encourages states to create novel and persuasive methods of child support enforcement in every state.

Child support collections on behalf of TANF recipients are kept by federal and state agencies in order to reimburse TANF distributions. Since 1989, however, there have been more non-welfare than welfare families in the CSE caseload, though a large amount (about forty-three percent) of cases do involve former TANF recipients. Because the number of TANF cases has fallen since the mid-1990s, when TANF became time-limited, more child support collections are going directly to custodial parents and fewer represent reimbursements for TANF payments. Thus by 2009, the federal government was losing nearly three billion dollars annually on the CSE program.[12]

Getting tough on child support collection is a popular idea with nearly all children's advocates, and has few critics save some fathers' groups concerned about exacerbating male – especially minority male – poverty and legal jeopardy. The idea has been affirmed, both in Secretary Hillary Rodham Clinton's well-known book, *It Takes a Village*,[13] and in Professor John Witte's history of illegitimacy law: *The Sins of the Fathers*.[14] Evidence indicates that, in addition to its positive income effects, the establishment and enforcement of child support may help connect fathers to their children, and even lower multi-partner fertility.[15]

Never-married mothers may have additional difficulties and complexities garnering child support because of their greater likelihood of multi-partner fertility, with all that this portends for fathers' hesitancy to support other men's children, and the requirement that the mother maintain more than one child support order. Multi-partner fertility is greatest among those women who have had their first birth outside of marriage, including women who were cohabiting when they give birth. A 2014 article reported that sixty percent of twenty-five- to thirty-two-year-old mothers with multi-partner fertility were neither cohabiting nor married at the time of their first birth.[16]

[12] Id., 4.
[13] Hillary Rodham Clinton, *It Takes a Village: And Other Lessons Children Teach Us* (New York: Touchstone, 1996).
[14] John Witte, *The Sins of the Fathers: The Law and Theology of Illegitimacy Reconsidered* (Cambridge: Cambridge University Press, 2009).
[15] Irwin Garfinkel et al., "The Role of Child Support Enforcement and Welfare in Non-Marital Childbearing," *Journal of Population Economics* 16 (2003): 55–70.
[16] Karen Benjamin Guzzo, "New Partners, More Kids: Multiple-Partner Fertility in the United States," *The American Academy of Political and Social Science* 654 (July 2014): 66–86.

Food

The leading federal program supplying food to those in need based upon family income and composition[17] is the Supplemental Nutrition Assistance Program ("SNAP"). Formerly known as the "food stamp" program, a program like SNAP has formally been in existence since 1964. It has grown to feed about forty-three million Americans, down from a high of almost forty-eight million in 2013. In 2014, the number of children in single-parent and unmarried partner homes receiving SNAP totaled 9.8 million, as distinguished from 5.2 million in married homes.[18] Seventy-one percent of SNAP proceeds go to households with children. Fifty-one percent of these households are single-parent families[19] About forty-six percent of single mothers receive food stamps. The federal government's SNAP webpage features a picture of a single mother with a child. Its total expenditures in 2016 neared seventy-one billion dollars.[20]

The federal government also sponsors a food program for pregnant, postpartum and lactating women and infants. It is called the Special Supplemental Nutrition Program for Women, Infants and Children (WIC) and provides grants to states for certain foods, health care referrals and nutrition education for pregnant and new mothers, and infants and children up to age five at risk for poor nutrition. Begun in 1974, by 2016, WIC served 7.7 million persons and cost about 6.9 billion dollars, of which nearly two billion dollars were administrative costs.[21]

The federal government also helps to feed children when they are not at home, in both public and private institutions including schools, day cares and camps. The National School Lunch Program ("NSLP") was begun in 1946 to provide breakfasts and lunches at schools and residential childcare institutions, for children through age eighteen. Meals are free for children at some incomes near or below poverty, and reduced-price for children at

[17] US Department of Agriculture, *Supplemental Nutrition Assistance Program*, www.fns.usda.gov/snap/supplemental-nutrition-assistance-program-snap; US Department of Agriculture, *Supplemental Nutrition Assistance Program (SNAP): Eligibility*, www.fns.usda.gov/snap/eligibility.

[18] US Department of Agriculture, Supplemental Nutrition Assistance Program (SNAP): A *Short History of SNAP*, www.fns.usda.gov/snap/short-history-snap.

[19] US Department of Agriculture, *Building a Healthy America: A Profile of the Supplemental Nutrition Assistance Program*, April 2012, www.fns.usda.gov/sites/default/files/BuildingHealthyAmerica.pdf.

[20] US Department of Agriculture, *Supplemental Nutrition Program Participation and Costs*, January 6, 2017, www.fns.usda.gov/sites/default/files/pd/SNAPsummary.pdf.

[21] US Department of Agriculture, *WIC Program and Participation Costs*, January 6, 2017, www.fns.usda.gov/sites/default/files/pd/wisummary.pdf.

slightly higher incomes. In 2012 the NSLP fed more than 31 million children in 100,000 institutions at a cost of nearly 12 billion dollars annually.[22] In 2016, the school lunch, school breakfast and milk programs cost the federal government about 18 billion dollars annually.[23] NSLP benefits are available to any family receiving SNAP. It was expanded in 1988 to cover after-school programs. Summer meals may also be covered, and in 2016, these were provided at nearly 48,000 sites at a cost of 474 million dollars.[24]

The Child and Adult Care Food Program (CACFP) specifically provides food for childcare (family or group day care homes) and at-risk after school care facilities for over three million children. Today it is provided to about two million persons, homes and centers at a cost of 3.5 billion dollars.[25]

Housing

The Federal government provides approximately 50 billion dollars annually in housing assistance for low-income families. This figure has remained fairly stable since 2003.[26] The assistance is provided most often through agency programs or tax benefits. According to the Congressional Budget Office, approximately 9.8 million people receive federal housing benefits – or about three percent of the population.[27]

Programs vary, and either allow recipients to pay for housing of their choice in the private market, or receive rent subsidies for private rentals, or obtain "Section 8" housing at a federally subsidized rental rate in buildings which are publicly owned and operated.[28] Most of the programs are administered by the Department of Housing and Urban Development,[29] although the Department of Agriculture also provides rural rental assistance.[30] A Low Income Housing

---

[22] US Department of Agriculture, *Child Nutrition Programs, National School Lunch Program*, September 2013, www.fns.usda.gov/sites/default/files/NSLPFactSheet.pdf.

[23] US Department of Agriculture, *Federal Cost of School Food Programs*, January 6, 2017, www.fns.usda.gov/sites/default/files/pd/cncost.pdf.

[24] US Department of Agriculture, *Summer Food Service Program*, January 6, 2017, www.fns .usda.gov/sites/default/files/pd/sfsummar.pdf.

[25] US Department of Agriculture, *Child and Adult Care Food Program*, January 6, 2017, www .fns.usda.gov/cacfp/afterschool-programs.

[26] Congressional Budget Office Report, *Federal Housing Assistance for Low-Income Households*, September 9, 2015, www.cbo.gov/publication/50782.

[27] *Id*. at 3.

[28] *Id*. at 5–7.

[29] Ehren Dohler et al., "Supportive Housing Helps Vulnerable People Live and Thrive in the Community," Center on Budget and Policy Priorities, May 31, 2016, www.cbpp.org/research/housing/supportive-housing-helps-vulnerable-people-live-and-thrive-in-the-community.

[30] Ibid.

Tax Credit is an indirect benefit to low-income citizens, and incentivizes developers to build less expensive housing.

The Congressional Budget Office reports that not much is known about the characteristics of households receiving federal housing assistance. Federal rules stipulate that recipients must have an income equal to thirty percent of the area median, or below – which varies from place to place. Beyond that, discretion regarding recipients is delegated to local public housing authorities. Approximately thirty-nine percent of households receiving assistance are households with children.[31]

A special federal program managed by the United States Department of Housing and Urban Development is called "Moving to Opportunity." Authorized in 1992, it provides rental assistance vouchers, and housing search assistance in order to help lower income families to move to neighborhoods with less poverty, and better educational, employment and social opportunities. It responds to research (described in Chapter Two) indicating that especially younger children can benefit from living in neighborhoods with a lower share of one-parent households, less segregation by income and race, better schools, and less violent crime.[32] At the beginning of the program, 4,600 low-income families, the vast majority headed by minority single mothers, were recruited in five cities between 1994 and 1998. A report commissioned by the responsible federal office found no effects on participants' education, employment, or income, and only modest health effects, both physical and psychological. The participants did perceive greater safety.[33]

Health Insurance

The federal government, in partnership with the states, also provides health insurance to the poor. The leading program is Medicaid. Before the Affordable Care Act was passed in 2010, Medicaid served only children, parents, pregnant women, people with disabilities and seniors; under the new act it is available to any adult between nineteen and sixty-five with certain income levels. It offers a sliding scale payment option based upon the recipient's income, up

[31] Congressional Budget Office, "Federal Housing Assistance for Low Income Households," Congressional Budget Office Report (September, 2015): 10, 43, www.fns.usda.gov/sites/default/files/NSLPFactSheet.pdf.

[32] US Department of Housing and Urban Development, "Moving to Opportunity for Fair Housing Demonstration Program: Final Impacts Evaluation," by Lisa Sanbonmatsu, U.S. Department of Housing and Urban Development, November, 2011, www.huduser.gov/publications/pdf/mtofhd_fullreport_v2.pdf.

[33] Ibid.

to four times poverty level. Medicaid expenditures for contraception will be treated separately, below.

For pregnant women, new mothers and young children, the federal government also offers a home visiting program. HHS administers this. Since 2010 it has been called the Maternal, Infant and Early Childhood Home Visiting Program (MIECHV). There are many different models eligible for federal funding. The program can provide at-risk families – low-income, pregnant women under twenty-one, families with a history of neglect or abuse, and others – voluntary home visits beginning early during a pregnancy and continuing generally until the child is five years old. Seventy-seven percent of the families had incomes at or below 100 percent of the federal poverty guidelines. Thirty-one percent of the adults possessed less than a high school diploma, and twenty-five percent more had a high school diploma. Sixty-eight percent belonged to a racial or ethnic minority. The programs can teach parenting skills, promote positive interactions and a language-rich environment, promote healthy behaviors, conduct health screenings, and link families to other community services. It seeks to assist both the mother's and the child's overall health, to prevent injuries and abuse, to promote school readiness, to reduce violence and to improve economic self-sufficiency, among other goals.[34] Its fiscal 2017 budget is 372 million dollars.[35]

In fiscal year 2015 the program served over 145 thousand parents and children in all fifty states, and in the District of Columbia, and in five territories. The government estimates that it has provided more than 2.3 million home visits between 2012 and 2015. Studies link this program causally with better health for mothers and children, safer home environments, and improved cognitive and social outcomes for children.[36] It regularly earns plaudits from politicians and policy experts, and from both the right and the left.[37]

---

[34] US Department of Health and Human Services, *The Maternal, Infant, and Early Childhood Home Visiting Program: Partnering with Parents to Help Children Succeed*, www.mchb.hrsa. gov/sites/default/files/mchb/MaternalChildHealthInitiatives/HomeVisiting/pdf/programbrief. pdf; US Department of Health and Human Services, *2016 MIECHV Formula Grant Funding Opportunity Announcement*, HRSA-16–172 Technical Assistance Webinar, December 10, 2015, www.mchb.hrsa.gov/sites/default/files/mchb/MaternalChildHealthInitiatives/HomeVisiting/ tafiles/transcript1215.pdf.

[35] US Department of Health and Human Services, *Home Visiting*, www.mchb.hrsa.gov/maternal-child-health-initiatives/home-visiting-overview.

[36] Edward Rodrigue and Richard V. Reeves, "Home visiting programs: an early test for the 114th Congress," Brookings Social Mobility Papers, February 5, 2015, www.brookings.edu/research/home-visiting-programs-an-early-test-for-the-114th-congress/.

[37] US Department of Health and Human Services, Home Visiting Evidence of Effectiveness: Implementing Family Check-Up for Children, August 2015, www.homvee.acf.hhs.gov/ Implementation/3/Family-Check-Up-For-Children-Implementation/9.

For children ages two to seventeen, there is another federally funded program called Family Check Up, which provides home visits by trained parent consultants to motivate mothers of at-risk children (at risk because of low SES, maternal depression and other family and child risk factors such as single-parenthood) to provide certain child management practices in order to help the child's self-regulation, pro-social behavior, and decision making respecting peers, alcohol, tobacco and drugs. It also attempts to improve maternal depression, parental involvement and positive parenting. Experts sometimes videotape parent-child interactions involving playing, helping, delaying gratification and teaching. For adolescents, the program provides a consultant at local schools offering screenings and interventions to assist with a child's competencies and mental health, among other services. The average cost per family per year is between 200 and 300 dollars annually, and the program has been evaluated as producing modestly favorable results in children's school-readiness, maternal health and positive parenting practices.[38]

Education

The federal government provides enormous resources – often in partnership with the states – to support education, including special programs and services for low-income children. A great deal of funding and good will and even national expectation is invested in educational programs with the hope that they might assist disadvantaged children to "catch up" with their more advantaged peers.

A substantial portion of the government's education programs are responding to the research about the importance of early brain development and the influence of parents upon it (Chapter Two). One sees in the federal materials, explicit references to the research of Betty Hart and Todd Risley[39] about dramatic word gaps between households by age three, and funding explicitly targeted to "bridging the word gap."[40] The Department Of Education has an Office of Early Learning overseeing a large number of programs directed to improving children's "health, socio-emotional, and cognitive

[38] US Department of Health and Human Services, *Implementing Family Check-Up for Children, Evidence of Program Model Effectiveness*, July 2011, www.homvee.acf.hhs.gov/Model/1/Family-Check-Up-For-Children-In-Brief/9.

[39] Hart and Risley, *Meaningful Differences in the Everyday Experience of Young American Children*.

[40] US Department of Health and Human Services, "Bridging the Word Gap Research Network" (NCHB grant #UA6MC27762), www.mchb.hrsa.gov/research/project_info.asp?ID=267.

outcomes" from birth through third grade, so that especially children with risk factors such as poverty or single-parenthood are able to enter high school "college-and-career-ready."

Early Head Start ("EHS") is a federally funded child development program, begun in 1994 as an extension of Head Start. It promotes healthy prenatal outcomes, infants' and toddlers' health, cognitive and language development, socio-emotional wellbeing, and supportive parent-child relationships. Local EHS agencies offer services in centers, and in homes. In 2006, EHS served over 61,000 children at a cost of about 10,500 dollars per child, for a total expenditure of over 6 billion dollars annually.[41]

A 2010 comprehensive evaluation[42] of the results of Early Head Start commissioned by the responsible federal office, showed both positive and negative outcomes relative to a control group of children and families who did not experience EHS. Depending upon the risk category of the parents (e.g., single-parent or low socioeconomic status) post-EHS outcomes were sometimes a bit better for children and worse for parents, or better for children in some arenas – for example, emotion – while worse in others, such as cognitive skills. Particularly negative impacts were noted among children in the highest-risk families compared to those in the control group.

Overall, however, in comparing the EHS Participants to the control group, the study detected significant impacts on the full sample of children for social-emotional functioning. However, there was variability between subgroups (by race or by venue, meaning home or center) regarding the duration of improvements. The study's authors recommended further research to help programs devise ways to engage highest-risk families more effectively.

For children between ages three and five, the federal government offers Head Start. Head Start aspires "to promote the school readiness of low-income children by enhancing their cognitive, social, and emotional development"[43] through education, health, social and other services. It employs social,

---

[41] Julia Issacs and Emily Roessel, "Impacts of Early Childhood Programs, Research Brief #3: Early Head Start," The Brookings Institution (2007), www.brookings.edu/wp-content/uploads/2016/07/09_early_programs_brief3.pdf.

[42] Office of Planning, Research, and Evaluation, US Department of Health and Human Services, *Early Head Start Children in Grade 5: Long-Term Follow-Up of the Early Head Start Research and Evaluation Study Sample*, by Cheri A. Vogel et al., Office of Planning, Research, and Evaluation, Administration for Children and Families, U.S. Department of Health and Human Services (OPRE Report # 2011–8, 2010).

[43] US Department of Health and Human Services, www.eclkc.ohs.acf.hhs.gov/hslc/standards/law/HS_Act_2007.pdf; see also Grover J. Russ Whitehurst, "Can We Be Hard-Headed About Preschool? A Look at Head Start," Brookings Institution Reports, January 16, 2013, www.brookings.edu/research/can-we-be-hard-headed-about-preschool-a-look-at-head-start/#_ftn7.

emotional, language and literacy training, and can also supply health care, dental and mental health services.

Head Start can operate in dedicated centers, other child-care centers and homes, and offers weekly visits in order to work with parents who are their child's primary teacher. It can offer support to parents regarding their housing needs, continued education, financial security, parent–child relationships, and parents' engagement with their child's learning. Depending upon a state's programs, Head Start may offer all-day or even year-round services. It was conceived as part of the War on Poverty in 1965, and by 2015 had served over thirty million children. Eighty percent of its participants are three- and four-year old children. There are 1,700 local agencies administering Head Start, located in every state, in U.S. territories, in farmworker camps and in tribal communities. Head Start's 2015 budget was 8.6 billion dollars.[44]

Regarding its efficacy, a widely cited 2012 evaluation commissioned by the responsible federal office concluded that, "by the end of third grade there were very few impacts ... in any of the four domains of cognitive, social-emotional, health and parenting practices. The few impacts that were found did not show a clear pattern of favorable or unfavorable impacts for children."[45] A 2016 study of a similar experiment in the United Kingdom, albeit involving universal preschool beginning at age 3, concluded that, while there were small improvements in children's educational attainment by age 5, these gains had disappeared by age 11.[46] One pre-school expert proposes that Head Start's annual 8 billion dollar budget would assist children to a greater degree were it used to provide additional income for low-income parents, plus preschool for all.[47]

It is fair to say that there is unease among supporters of Head Start given not only disappointing results in the United States, but also disappointing results of similar programs in other countries. Many experts have proposed ideas for improving or standardizing Head Start, particularly given its varying forms across states. Proposals abound involving different structures, better-prepared teachers, and varying academic content.

---

[44] US Department of Health and Human Services, *Early Childhood Learning and Knowledge Center, Head Start Program Facts*, Fiscal Year 2015, www.eclkc.ohs.acf.hhs.gov/hslc/data/factsheets/2015-hs-program-factsheet.html.

[45] US Department of Health and Human Services, *Third Grade Follow-Up to the Head Start Impact Study: Final Report*, U.S. Department of Health and Human Services (OPRE Report 2012–45, 2012), www.acf.hhs.gov/sites/default/files/opre/head_start_report.pdf.

[46] Jo Blanden, et al., "Universal Pre-school Education: The Case of Public Funding with Private Provision," *The Economic Journal* 126 (2016): 682–723.

[47] Grover J. Russ Whitehurst, "Family support or school readiness?" Brookings Report, April 28, 2016.

Pre-school enthusiasts continue to point with near reverence to two projects which appeared to create long run benefits for poor and frequently nonmarital children who participated four to five decades ago: the Abcedarian Project and the High/Scope Perry Preschool Project. The first, begun in 1972, provided high quality all-day and year-round preschool and educational child care to children between nought and five in 120 disadvantaged families – seventy-five percent of whom were single-parent homes. The teacher–child ratio ranged from 1:3 for infants to 1:6 for five-year-olds. In 2013, the average annual cost was 18,000 dollars per child. The second program offered one or two years of preschool education to 123 poor three- and four-year-old African-American children from a distressed neighborhood in Michigan, between 1962 and 1967. There were four certified teachers for twenty-five children, 2.5 hours per day, five days per week. The teachers also visited each child and his or her mother for 1.5 hours per week. The program cost approximately 11,300 dollars annually per child in 2007 dollars.[48]

In both cases, results were promising. The children from one or both projects experienced better long-term employment and educational outcomes, fewer criminal records, fewer nonmarital births and later first childbirth.

Not a few education experts wish to replicate these two projects. Other commentators point to the high costs and small sample sizes of both projects, and are skeptical that they can be the basis for future large-scale government programs.[49] But state experiments continue apace, sometimes with better outcomes than Head Start.[50]

A significant number of education scholars are increasingly requesting that the government focus upon raising teachers' competencies in order to raise student outcomes. The competencies they identify increasingly resemble what are often considered parenting skills. For examples, experts recommend that teachers be better prepared to instruct children regarding: social and emotional self-regulation, the boundaries of appropriate behavior, how to interact with other children, how to prevent bullying, and how to demonstrate tolerance. They also recommend that teachers raise students' academic

[48] Coalition for Evidence Based Policy, Social Programs that Work: The Perry Preschool Project, www.evidencebasedprograms.org/1366-2/65-2; Coalition for Evidence Based Policy, Social Programs That Work: The Abecedarian Project, www.evidencebasedprograms.org/1366-2/abecedarian-project.

[49] Michael Q. McShane, "Media draw big misleading conclusions from a study with a small sample size," *The National Review*, December 16, 2016, www.nationalreview.com/article/436794/uk-preschool-study-finds-no-educational-gains-expanded-programs.

[50] Tomoko Wakabayashi, et al., "High-quality, statewide preschool is possible-just look to Michigan," Brookings Institution Report, January 25, 2017, www.brookings.edu/blog/brown-center-chalkboard/2017/01/25/high-quality-statewide-preschool-is-possible-just-look-to-michigan/.

aspirations, give more personal tutoring to students, and craft more rigorous curricula. Because of the additional demands this imposes on teachers, experts further recommend raising teacher salaries and teaching teachers how to better handle stress.

Other experts urge government to better integrate home and school, especially to boost parents' ability to help their children and to harmonize expectations for behavior at home and in school. They also recommend integrating educational programming for parents with training for teachers, more parent–teacher meetings, more interventions with parents to help them raise children's educational expectations, and improving parents' capacities to communicate guidance and support.

Pointing to the disappointing and even dismal results of prior efforts to boost parents' school involvement, some experts are instead proposing that government should simply increase parents' income and help them better balance work and family.[51]

Federal education programs also attend to homeless children, many of whom are being reared by single mothers. In 2007, a survey by the U.S. Conference of Mayors found that sixty-five percent of homeless adults who are accompanied by family are women.[52] The McKinney-Vento Education of Homeless Children and Youth Assistance Act is a federal law requiring immediate enrollment and educational stability for homeless children and youth; it provides federal funding to states for programs serving homeless students.

There is also a federal program to eliminate chronic absenteeism among at-risk children, many of whom are poor and living in single parent homes. It is called Every Student, Every Day, and is targeted to the most vulnerable children, including those attending the most low performing schools.[53] The program is a key part of President Obama's "My Brothers Keeper" Initiative,[54] begun by the president with a very personal appeal to "young men of color"

---

[51] See generally, Nonie K. Lesaux and Stephanie M. Jones, *The Leading Edge of Early Childhood Education: Linking Science to Policy for a New Education* (Cambridge: Harvard Education Press, Cambridge: 2016); Bruce Bradbury et al., *Too Many Children Left Behind, the U.S. Achievement Gap in Comparative Perspective*, (New York: Russell Sage Foundation, 2015); and Greg J. Duncan and Richard J. Murnane, eds. *Whither Opportunity?:Rising Inequality, Schools, and Children's Life Chances* (New York: Russell Sage Foundation, 2011).

[52] National Coalition for the Homeless, Who Is Homeless? (July 2009) at www.nationalhomeless.org/factsheets/Whois.pdf.

[53] US Department of Education, *Every Student, Every Day: A National Initiative to Address and Eliminate Chronic Absenteeism*, www2.ed.gov/about/inits/ed/chronicabsenteeism/index.html.

[54] US Department of Education, *My Brother's Keeper*, www2.ed.gov/about/inits/ed/earlylearning/initiatives.html#mbk.

at a press conference in 2014, and with special attention to single-parent homes lacking father involvement. During the president's inaugural address on the subject, he spoke plainly about his own fatherless upbringing, and about the worse social outcomes faced by young men of color reared without their fathers. He claimed that "nothing keeps a young man out of trouble like a father who takes an active role in his son's life" and referred to well-fathered children likely becoming "better husbands and fathers" themselves.[55] The program focuses on six life "milestones:" pre-school cognitive, physical social, and emotional competence; grade-level reading at third and eighth grade; high school skills sufficient for postsecondary education or training; college opportunity; jobs; and education and training opportunities for ex-convicts.

The Federal TRIO Programs, available since 1968, are designed to help low-income and "disadvantaged" young people, and first-generation college students to complete high school and college. They have several components. Students are helped to select post-secondary education and obtain financial aid, boost math and science accomplishment, and access campus-based child-care. Total funding in 2016 was: 275 million dollars for student support services for 205,000 students; 155 million dollars for talent search for 306,000 students; and nearly 50 million dollars for assisting 73,000 students in math and science.[56]

The federal government is also involved in providing education to adults to develop basic skills necessary to function in society, to finish secondary school, and to experience enhanced family life.[57] The United States Department of Education provides grants to states for local programs for adult education and literacy for those of sixteen and older. This can include instruction in reading, numeracy, and preparation for a General Education Diploma (GED) certificate.[58] The Adult Education and Family Literacy Act also tries to provide workers and job seekers seamless access to a system of high-quality career services, education, and training through the one-stop service delivery system,

[55] Barack Obama, Remarks by the President on 'My Brother's Keeper' Initiative, February 27, 2014, www.whitehouse.gov/the-press-office/2014/02/27/remarks-president-my-brothers-keeper-initiative.

[56] US Department of Education, *Federal Trio Programs*, www2.ed.gov/about/offices/list/ope/trio/index. html#news; US Department of Education, Fiscal Year 2017 budget: Summary and Background Information, www2.ed.gov/about/overview/budget/budget17/summary/17summary.pdf.

[57] US Department of Education, Office of Career, Technical and Adult Education, www2 .ed.gov/about/offices/list/ovae/index.html.

[58] US Department of Education, Basic Grants to States, www2.ed.gov/programs/adultedbasic/ index.html.

known as the American Job Centers, and partners. Its 2016 budget was 595 million dollars.[59]

The federal Child Care and Development Fund (CCDF) has provided child care support to low-income working families since 1990, including for direct services as well as for quality enhancements to existing services. The majority of CCDF dollars are used to provide subsidies to low-income children under age thirteen. In 2016 it served 1.4 million children from 850,000 low-income families using 340,000 childcare providers. It spends about 5 billion dollars annually.[60]

For family members over fifty-five, caring for children under eighteen, there has been a National Family Caregiver Support Program since 1965.[61] Twelve percent of its recipients were caring for a grandson or daughter. The federal budget in 2011 was about 154 million dollars.

Employment

The federal government has funded training and employment programs for vulnerable youth since the 1930s. These programs expanded during both the New Deal and the War on Poverty. Today, they are largely administered by the Department of Labor.

Under the Workforce Investment Act, job training is offered through locally administered boards. In fiscal year 2015, one billion dollars was expended. Job Corps provides training in various trades; 1.7 billion dollars was expended in fiscal year 2015. YouthBuild provides education and job training in the construction field, and spent about 89 million dollars in 2015. The Reintegration of Ex-Offenders Program provides job training for juvenile offenders, and spent 44.1 million dollars in 2015.[62]

An evaluation of Job Corps by respected analyst Mathematica reported that Job Corps was a modest success. It appeared to increase educational or training attainments, and reduce criminal activity. Earnings gains were not sustained over several years, however, save for the oldest members of the group.

[59] US Department of Education, Fiscal Year 2017 Budget: Summary and Background Information, www2.ed.gov/about/overview/budget/budget17/summary/17summary.pdf.

[60] US Department of Health and Human Services, Final Rule: Frequently Asked Questions (December 14, 2016), www.acf.hhs.gov/occ/resource/ccdf-final-rule-faq.

[61] US Department of Health and Human Services, National Family Caregiver Support Program, www.aoa.acl.gov/AoA_Programs/HCLTC/Caregiver/.

[62] Martha Ross and Richard Kazis, "Renew the federal commitment to high-quality summer youth employment programs," Brookings Report 4 (2016), www.brookings.edu/wp-content/uploads/2016/10/ross-kazis-briefv5-002.pdf.

The study noted that Job Corps is the only federal training program that has been shown to increase earnings at all for the population it serves.

Marriage

Another well-known federal program involves providing education to individuals and couples about the following subjects: the benefits of marriage and two-parent involvement for children; relationship skills; controlling aggressive behavior; causes of domestic violence and child abuse; marriage preparation and counseling; financial planning; and parenting skills, and payment of child support.[63]

The program was begun under President George W. Bush and continued by President Obama. The federal government offers grants to sponsors of various program-models. Some of the programs are directed to single persons, some to unmarried parents and some to already-married parents. Some paid special attention to low-income couples, and some were available to any interested couple. The Obama administration highlighted fatherhood programs to a greater degree, while continuing the marriage efforts.

Initially, the marriage programs were subject to criticism on the grounds of government ineptitude as a "matchmaker," or fears that the government would coerce a woman into a violent marriage, or on the grounds of general discomfort with marriage on the belief that it promotes role limitations for women. These concerns are not often heard in recent years, following the implementation of the programs.

As of 2017, both marriage and fatherhood programs are funded, together, at 150 million dollars annually, with fatherhood programs receiving 55 million dollars. These efforts are directed toward helping fathers find work in order to pay their child support, to help avoid further nonmarital births, to boost families' relationships, and to encourage two-parent families, though not necessarily marriage. Incarcerated men receive dedicated programming. Tools include media campaigns, parenting education, mediation and conflict resolution services, child support assistance, stress-relief and problem solving training, peer support and job services. Grants are distributed for projects running through fiscal year 2020. The fatherhood programs await further evaluation.[64]

---

[63] US Department of Health and Human Services, Healthy Marriage and Responsible Fatherhood, at www.acf.hhs.gov/ofa/programs/healthy-marriage.

[64] Carmen Solomon-Fears and Jessica Tollestrup, "Fatherhood Initiatives: Connecting Fathers to Their Children," Congressional Research Service (Report RL31025), December 28, 2016.

Evaluations of older fatherhood efforts similar to the programs funded today, however, show mixed results: some employment and income figures are disappointing, while a few are more promising. Some, but not all, programs produced increased numbers of established child support orders, or more payment of child support, or additional contact between fathers and children.[65]

At several junctures, the federal government has commissioned evaluations of its marriage programs. The Supporting Healthy Marriage initiative was directed at low-income married couples rearing or expecting a child. It included workshop, family support and community-connection elements, among others. A 2014 evaluation of the program's effectiveness since 2003 concluded that it did not lead more couples to stay together, and had little effect on co-parenting, parenting or child well-being. It also appeared to reduce women's but not men's sadness and worry, but had small positive effects nearly three years out on couples' happiness, fidelity and warmth.[66]

Building Strong Families is a federal program offering grants to relationship and education programs supporting unwed couples who are expecting or rearing a child together. It included group sessions (the most important aspect), individual support, and referrals to necessary services in areas like health or employment. Topics for discussion and support included communication, intimacy and trust, marriage, parenting. A 2012 evaluation[67] found no effect on relationship quality, stability or the decision to marry. It had no effect on co-parenting and a small negative effect on father involvement. Children's behavior was modestly better, although families' economic situations were not improved.

A program for military married couples, however – PREP for Strong Bonds – saw positive results for divorce rates and communications skills and couple reconciliation.

A Brookings Institute expert on family policy noted that[68] while these results are disappointing, it should be kept in mind that many government programs

---

[65] Ibid.

[66] US Department of Health and Human Services, *A Family-Strengthening Program for Low-Income Families: Final Impacts from the Supporting Healthy Marriage Evaluation*, by Amy E. Lowenstein, et al., US Department of Health and Human Services (OPRE Report 2014-09B), January 2014.

[67] US Department of Health and Human Services, *The Long Term Effects of Building Strong Families: A Relationship Skills Education Program for Unmarried Parents: Final Report*, by Robert G. Wood, U.S. Department of Health and Human Services, (OPRE Report 2012-28A), November 2012.

[68] Ron Haskins, "The Family Is Here to Stay – or Not," *The Future of Children* 25 (Fall 2015): 140–143.

fail to deliver impressive results at their very beginning, and require amendment over time.

SUMMARY AND CONCLUSION: BACK DOOR PROGRAMS

The scope of federal programs to assist disadvantaged children, young adults,
and their families is vast. Their variety, and the fact that low-income and single-
parent families take advantage of multiple programs, indicate how the problems of poverty, unemployment, parenting deficits, and related emotional,
cognitive, educational and behavioral problems may nest together in homes
regularly lacking a second, stably involved parent. These programs prevent a
great deal of misery, and seek to promote social justice. Yet they are not the
entire answer for children.

According to a much-cited article by Nobel economist James Heckman,[69]
while early investments pay big dividends – both for building children's capacity, and economically, for society – later investments do not. Referring to
investments in school programs, for example, he concludes that "later schooling and variations in schooling quality have little effect in reducing or widening the gaps that appear before students enter school." He adds that this
is likely due not only to their early family environments, which are "major
predictors" of cognitive and noncognitive skills, but also to the fact that, even
during school years "families ... are the major sources of inequality in student
performance." He also refers to the "track records" of federal job programs
and adult literacy as "remarkably poor" and urges that while later programs
have some benefits and can boost early gains, the most efficient, most effective
interventions are the earliest.

Family scholar Isabel Sawhill has remarked that she supports the "usual set
of safety-net programs. But we've been working on these programs for decades, and they're hard." She concludes that they cannot substitute for a strong
family, but rather "that for every child that you pull out of poverty with some
social program, you're going to find another child falling into poverty because
of the breakdown of the family."[70]

Increasingly, federal programs intervene into the heart of the family – into
private homes and into the personal dynamics between parent and child, and

---

[69] James J. Heckman, "Skill Formation and the Economics of Investing in Disadvantaged
Children," *Science* 312 (June 30, 2006): 1900–1902.
[70] Nathan Pippenger, "Arguments Q + A: Isabel Sawhill, Author of Generation Unbound,"
Democracy: A Journal of Ideas, October 17, 2014, www.democracyjournal.org/arguments/
arguments-qa-isabel-sawhill-author-of-generation-unbound/.

between father and mother. Some monitor and guide verbal interactions, parenting styles and other intrafamilial matters. They work to forge links between the mother and the father, between each parent and each child, between home and school, between children and their teachers and counselors, and eventually between older children and potential employers. Overall, they are trying to forge the links, and boost the skills that a well-functioning family might demonstrate. Of course, not all marital families are parenting ideally. Still, the size and scope of the federal programs are a testament to what stably connected and invested family units might do for children; and what nonmarital households stand to lose in the absence of such a second parent.

Harvard sociologist Pitrim Sorokim predicted in the mid-1950s that the loss of customary norms about sex, marriage and responsibility for children would lead to the growth of government, in part because society would be reluctant to correct course.[71] He was right. Just a little more than a decade later, the federal government opted – instead of correcting course – to try to stem poverty and nonmarital births with massive contraception programs. This is the subject of the next section.

CONTRACEPTION

The federal government relies a great deal upon contraception as a proposed solution to avoid nonmarital parenting, poverty or unintended pregnancies. While the government's messaging focuses first on the interests of the mother in avoiding "unintended pregnancy," its contraception efforts should be interpreted as addressing nonmarital parenting, if only because so many nonmarital births are unintended.

As described in more detail in Chapter One, especially during the Obama administration, the federal government's rhetoric about the good of contraception for women and the importance of easy access, was warm, emotional, and even dramatic. It regularly linked contraception with the values of freedom, opportunity and equality. It referred to efforts to attain conscience protection respecting contraception as a "war on women" and fought over 300 religious plaintiffs through the federal courts and twice up to the Supreme Court. President Obama and many members of Congress campaigned on contraception as a proxy for a "pro-woman" platform. The struggle over the contraception mandate featured all of these tendencies.

The strength of the federal commitment to contraception can also be gauged by continued federal enthusiasm in the face of contraception's decades'-long

---

[71] Pitirim A. Sorokin, *The American Sex Revolution* (Boston: Porter Sargent, 1956), 132–136.

failure to reduce unintended pregnancies or abortion, as detailed in Chapter One. Even state level contraception mandates have not succeeded on a local level. According to sociologist Michael New, who investigated abortion and unintended pregnancy rates in twenty-six states with contraception mandates, at the end of several years, these states had similar rates of unintended pregnancies as states without mandates, and slightly higher abortion rates.[72]

While this book is concerned with the federal stance on adults' sexual expression, it should be noted that federal authorities regularly claim that contraceptive programs have proved their efficacy by contributing to historic declines in teen pregnancy rates. This sustains hope that they might ultimately succeed respecting adults. A few words on this subject before returning to the matter of contraception programs for adults.

It is true that *teen* pregnancy rates in recent years are declining by large percentages. Respecting *nonmarital* pregnancies, however, the results are not as encouraging. In 1957, when teen pregnancy rates were at an all-time high, there were ninety-six births per 1,000 teens; but eighty-five percent of these were marital. This means there were about fourteen nonmarital pregnancies per 1,000 teens. Today, the figures are rather reversed: eighty-nine percent of the twenty-four pregnancies per 1,000 teen girls are *non*marital. This means we are experiencing 21.5 nonmarital births per 1,000 teens today, a fifty percent rise in the *non*marital teen birth rate since 1957.[73] Our current rate of nonmarital teen births is still far lower today than it was in the 1990s; but it does not represent a decline in nonmarital teen parenting over the last sixty years.

Returning to the matter of adult nonmarital birth rates and the federal response, the strength of the government's support for contraception is further indicated by the its funding research to achieve a wider variety of safer contraceptives, more acceptable to women, as noted in the National Institutes of Health request for proposal quoted below. It doesn't leave this work to the private pharmaceutical companies alone. Federal authorities also work to promote cheaper, faster and more accessible contraception for all women, but especially for poorer women, as will be described below.

Finally, the amount of funding available for contraception also showcases the degree of federal interest. In recent budget years, the federal government has spent over two billion dollars annually on contraception. Medicaid reimbursement for contraception provided to poor women constitutes the largest

[72] Michael J. New, "Analyzing the Impact of State Level Contraception Mandates on Public Health Incomes."
[73] Eileen Patten and Gretchen Livingston, "Why is the teen birth rate falling?" Pew Research Center: Facttank, April 29, 2016, www.pewresearch.org/fact-tank/2016/04/29/why-is-the-teen-birth-rate-falling/.

portion. The Title X birth control program, serving four million clients in 2015 – 88 percent of whom received it free or highly subsidized – is the next largest program.[74] Each of these will be described in greater detail below.

Turning to the programs themselves, for reasons of space, only the leading programs are described here, insofar as it is necessary to understand the relationship between federal contraception efforts, and the prevention of nonmarital births.

Medicaid

Medicaid insurance covers all Food and Drug Administration approved drugs and devices for women and girls of childbearing age. The federal Medicaid program reimburses doctors providing contraception at a 90 percent rate, while the reimbursement rate for other Medicaid services range from 50 to 70 percent. States often supply the last 10 percent of the cost for low-income women.[75]

Contraception also receives favored treatment with respect to a Medicaid patient's choice of providers. While Medicaid managed-care enrollees are usually restricted to network providers, for contraception, a woman can go to the provider of her choice, even if he or she is not "in network."

The ACA established a new optional Medicaid eligibility group for family planning services, consisting of individuals with incomes at or below the highest income eligibility level established by the state for pregnant women. This new eligibility group entitles members *only* to family planning services and supplies and related diagnoses and treatment. Providers must give services for free.[76]

As described in Chapter One, in 2016 Medicaid officials strongly recommended that providers step up their efforts to deliver more and more effective contraception to the poor. Medicaid guidelines to states and providers encourage the latter to "optimize" the use of LARCs by encouraging

---

[74] Adam Sonfield and Rachel Benson Gold, *Public Funding for Family Planning, Sterilization and Abortion Services*, FY 1980–2010 (Guttmacher Institute, 2012); US Centers for Disease Control, "Update: Providing Quality Family Planning Services – Recommendations from the CDC and the U.S. Office of Population Affairs, by Loretta Gavin and Karen Pazol, U.S. Centers for Disease Control, *Morbidity and Mortality Weekly Report* 65, no. 9 (March 11, 2016); 231–234.

[75] Guttmacher Institute, Publicly Funded Family Planning Services in the United States: Fact Sheet, September 2016, www.guttmacher.org/fact-sheet/publicly-funded-family-planning-services-united-states.

[76] Alison Mitchell, et al., "Medicaid: An Overview" A Congressional Research Service Report (Report R43357) (January 10, 2014).

patients to consider it at every visit, by stocking a substantial amount and variety of contraception in order to make same-day access possible, and by recommending the insertion of an IUD or another LARC immediately after a woman has completed her labor and delivery. Medicaid is also amending its reimbursement policies to facilitate doctors' adoption of each of these recommendations.[77]

Title X

The Title X family planning program was created in 1970 as part of the Public Health Service Act. It provides grants to public and nonprofit agencies for contraception services, and research and training for both adults and adolescents. This can also include natural family planning and infertility counseling, cancer screening and prevention; sexually transmitted infection (STI) and HIV prevention education, counseling, testing, and referral; preconception health services; and counseling about a reproductive life plan. Contraception is by far the largest element of Title X expenditures.

Today, Title X receives about 286 million dollars per year and serves four million clients, eighty-eight percent of whom received contraception free or highly subsidized. About nine out of every ten Title X users are female, 67 percent are under thirty, and 66 percent have family incomes at or below the poverty level. Clients are disproportionately black and Hispanic. Five-sixths of clients are 20 and older.[78]

Community Health Centers

Contraception is also supplied through the Federal Health Center Program, through outlets called Community Health Centers ("CHCs"). These provide outpatient health services, including contraception, to underserved areas.[79]

---

[77] US Department of Health and Human Services, Letter from Centers for Medicaid and Medicaid Services, to State Health Officials, June 14, 2016 (SHO # 16-008), www.medicaid.gov/federal-policy-guidance/downloads/sho16008.pdf.

[78] Angela Napilii, "Title X (Public Health Service Act) Family Planning Program," Congressional Research Service Report (Report RL 33644) (September 26, 2016), www.fas.org/sgp/crs/misc/RL33644.pdf.

[79] Elayne J. Heisler, "Federal Health Centers: An Overview," Congressional Research Service Report (Report R43937) (January 6, 2016), at www.fas.org/sgp/crs/misc/R43937.pdf; Elayne J. Heisler, "Factors Related to the Use of Planned Parenthood Affiliated Health Centers (PPAHCs) and Federally Qualified Health Centers (FQHCs)," Congressional Research Service Report (Report R44295) (December 3, 2015), at www.fas.org/sgp/crs/misc/R44295.pdf.

Maternal and Child Health Block Grants

HHS administers Maternal and Child Health Block Grants, which provide funds to states, territories, and the District of Columbia to support a wide range of social service activities, including contraception.

Emergency Contraception

In 2013, the federal Food and Drug Administration made certain forms of emergency contraception ("ECs") – drugs taken after sex either to avoid conception or to avoid an embryo embedding into the womb – available over the counter without a prescription, to women over the age of 17.[80]

The Contraception Mandate

Chapter One described the contraception mandate issued by HHS in pursuance of the "preventive health care" provision of the ACA. Despite two trips to the U.S. Supreme Court, and instructions from the Court in the second action to find a "less restrictive means" than relying upon religious employers' plans to deliver contraception, the federal Department of Justice was still seeking a way at the close of 2016 to require religious conscientious objectors to offer "seamless" and free contraception to their employees. At the time of writing, it appears likely that President Trump's executive order, advising HHS not to exact penalties for violations of the ACA, may herald the effective end of enforcement of the mandate.

Dissatisfaction and Health Effects

The National Institutes of Health, a research branch of the federal Department of Health and Human Services, has summarized the leading reasons why existing birth control programs are failing to satisfy federal goals. In 2014 it issued a request for proposals to develop new birth control methods using federal funds, saying:

> Despite the availability of multiple contraceptive options, 49% of pregnancies in the U.S. are unintended.... Although 62% of reproductive age women in the US are using contraception, the unintended pregnancy rates

---

[80] The US Food and Drug Administration, "FDA Approves Plan B One-Step Emergency Contraceptive for Use Without a Prescription for All Women of Child-bearing Potential," press release, June 20, 2013, www.fda.gov/NewsEvents/Newsroom/PressAnnouncements/ucm358082.htm.

and abortion rates continue to be high…. However, hormonal contraceptives have the disadvantage of having many undesirable side effects. In addition, hormonal contraceptives are associated with adverse events, and obese women are at higher risk for serious complications such as deep venous thrombosis. The oral contraceptive pill's failure rate among American women ranges from 9–30%. The reason for such a high failure rate is the requirement for daily compliance. Furthermore, a recent report found that 40% of women were not satisfied with their current contraceptive method…. Long-acting reversible contraception, which does not require daily compliance, has a much lower typical use failure rate. The perfect use and typical use failure percentages are very close for these methods. However, most of these methods are either devices, such as the IUD, or contain hormones. Use of intrauterine devices has only slowly gained acceptance in the US (from 0.8% in 1995 to 5.6% in 2006–2010), and IUDs are unlikely to be used by the majority of women desiring contraception. These statistics suggest there is a need to develop highly effective non-hormonal contraceptives that have fewer side effects than the currently available methods.[81]

The failure of federal contraceptive efforts was also summarized by an Institute of Medicine panel, convened for the sole purpose of proposing better solutions to unintended pregnancy:

Experts in contraception and family planning, as well as men and women themselves, have long noted that the existing array of methods is often ill suited to the varying needs of couples and individuals over time, and that some methods are too difficult or unpleasant to use consistently, while others are too expensive or unsatisfactory in some other way. This underlying discontent with current contraceptive technology is at the heart of repeated calls for expanded research to develop new forms of contraception.[82]

Exploring women's dissatisfaction with contraception further, a 2013 CDC report stated that: "Of the 45 million women who have ever used the pill, 30% discontinued use because of dissatisfaction. Nearly one-half of the 12.5 million women who had used Depo-Provera (46%) and the 5.6 million women who had used the contraceptive patch (49%) discontinued use due to dissatisfaction."[83]

---

[81] US Department of Health and Human Services, Female Contraceptive Development Program (U01) (November 5, 2013), www.grants.nih.gov/grants/guide/rfa-files/RFA-HD-14-024.html (accessed February 1, 2017).

[82] Institute of Medicine, *The Best Intentions: Unintended Pregnancy and the Well Being of Children and Families* (Washington, DC: The National Academies Press, 1995), 127.

[83] US Centers for Disease Control, *Contraception Methods Women Have Ever Used: United States, 1982–2010*, by Kimberly Daniels, et al., U.S. Centers for Disease Control (February 14, 2013), www.cdc.gov/nchs/data/nhsr/nhsr062.pdf.

The NIH summary above also referred to contraception's health effects. From time to time – and especially in the context of the contraception mandate debate, or after widespread reports of a study reporting adverse health effects – the federal government and some of its grantees and partners will highlight the health benefits of birth control. These are often stated as: reducing menstrual disorders, acne, hirsutism (excess hair), and pelvic pain.[84] Regarding cancer, while the federal government stresses contraception's possible benefits for endometrial and ovarian cancer,[85] according to the American Cancer Society, the evidence is more mixed. They report that there is "consistent" evidence that hormonal birth control may reduce the above cancer risks, while at the same time increasing a woman's risk of breast and cervical cancer.[86]

Regarding additional negative health effects, reports will often receive breathless media coverage, but do not generally interfere with women's willingness to use contraception. Still, the reported negative effects are not negligible. The NIH summary above referred to the risks of serious adverse events such as blood clots and strokes for women who are obese: thirty-six percent of American women are obese.[87] Federal factsheets also regularly warn women over thirty-five who smoke to avoid hormonal birth control. They also report a link between hormonal contraception and blood clots and strokes for all women, especially in connection with newer progesterone products, but only in connection with post-partum women.[88] Others' accounts of the risks of blood clots and strokes are not restricted to the same limited class of women.

For example, well-publicized lawsuits linking hormonal contraceptives with strokes for other groups of women continue to create unease. Over the past several decades, for example, Bayer Pharmaceuticals have paid nearly two billion dollars to settle a class action lawsuit involving forms of the pill. Merck Pharmaceuticals paid 100 million dollars to settle a lawsuit involving 3,800 women, and eighty-three deaths, claimed to be linked to its Nuva Ring product[89] The Food and Drug Administration and the manufacturer of Depo

[84] Institute of Medicine, *Clinical Preventive Services for Women: Closing the Gaps* (Washington, DC: The National Academies Press, 2011), 107.

[85] Ibid.

[86] Kelli Miller, Birth Control and Cancer: Which Methods Raise, Lower Risk, The American Cancer Society, January 21, 2016, www.cancer.org/cancer/news/features/birth-control-cancer-which-methods-raise-lower-risk.

[87] US Department of Health and Human Services, Overweight and Obesity Statistics, www.niddk.nih.gov/health-information/health-statistics/Pages/overweight-obesity-statistics.aspx.

[88] US Department of Health and Human Services, Birth control methods, www.womenshealth.gov/node/656/birth-control-methods.

[89] Melisssa Brumer, "Merck's $100 Million NuvaRing Settlement: Is Merck 'Getting Off Easy'?" *The Jurist*, March 22, 2014: Amanda Anteli, "Bayer Pays Out $1.4 Billion in Yaz Lawsuit

Provera (Pfizer), an injected hormonal birth control – warn users in bold language about the drug's links with bone loss, especially among young women. The federal *womenshealth.gov* website states, for example, that Depo Provera "should not be used more than 2 years in a row" because "it can cause a temporary loss of bone density," which grows over time. It also cautioned that, while the "bone does start to grow after this method is stopped … it may increase the risk of fracture and osteoporosis if used for a long time."[90]

Evidence about a link between Depo Provera and increased HIV transmission has also circulated for over twenty-five years.[91] A 2012 study created the most significant alarm.[92] Currently, even though the World Health Organization has decided to continue recommending Depo Provera (albeit combined with a condom), there remain significant scientific concerns[93] that it facilitates HIV transmission. Any mention of this risk is absent from the contraception factsheet that the federal government offers to the public. But the National Institutes' of Health Contraceptive Development Program has awarded nearly 500,000 dollars each year from 2013 to 2018 for the study of possible mechanisms by which Depo Provera might increase HIV transmission.[94]

There is furthermore a credible literature that hormonal birth control may alter women's partner preferences in a way disadvantageous to the stability of a relationship after the woman ceases using the pill.[95] Another important study from 2014 issued a "strong demand" for more studies investigating evidence of the ways in which hormonal contraceptives affect the human brain from the molecular to the behavioral level. It summarizes existing research showing

---

Settlements," Top Class Actions (October 2, 2013), www.topclassactions.com/lawsuit-settlements/prescription/5008-bayer-pays-out-1-4-billion-in-yaz-lawsuit-settlements/.

[90] US Department of Health and Human Services, Birth control methods; Pfizer, Medical Information: Depo Provera, www.womenshealth.gov/node/656/birth-control-methods.

[91] Chelsea B. Polis, "Hormonal contraceptive methods and risk of HIV acquisition in women: a systematic review of epidemiological evidence," *Contraception* 90 (2014): 360–390.

[92] Renee Heffron et al., "Hormonal contraceptive use and risk of HIV-1 transmission: a prospective cohort analysis," *The Lancet* 12 (2012): 19–26.

[93] Lauren J. Ralph, "Hormonal contraceptive use and women's risk of HIV acquisition: a meta-analysis of observational studies," *The Lancet* 15 (February 2015): 181–189.

[94] US Department of Health and Human Services, Research Grants, Tilton, John Christian, Case Western Reserve University, "Enhancement of HIV Transmission By Hormones And Bacterial Metabolites" ("The goal of the proposed research project is to define how hormonal variation during the normal menstrual cycle (endogenous hormones) and with DMPA contraceptives (synthetic progestin) and bacterial vaginosis affect protein expression in ectocervical CD4+ T lymphocytes and their susceptibility to fusion and productive infection with HIV."), www.grantome.com/grant/NIH/R01-HD077886-02.

[95] Anthony C. Little, "Oral contraceptive use in women changes preferences for male facial masculinity and is associated with partner facial masculinity," *Psychoneuroendocrinology* 38 (September 2013): 1777–1785.

that contraceptive hormones have both feminizing and masculinizing effects; that they appear to affect both brain structure and function; that caution is warranted during "sensitive neuroplastic periods during puberty;" and that noted changes in personality and social behavior might portend larger social consequences.[96]

Women have also complained of a link between the pill and depression since the well-known "pill hearings" of the 1970s. A 2016 study,[97] is the most noted and current research about a possible link between depression and hormonal contraception. The peer-reviewed study found that, among one million women in a Danish register linkage database – ages 15 to 34, and without a prior history of depression or other major psychiatric disorders – users of hormonal contraceptives were, on average, 23 percent more likely than non-users to be using prescribed anti-depressants, or diagnosed with depression. Much higher chances of depression were found among women using the contraceptive patch (100 percent) the "ring," (60 percent) and the hormonal IUD (40 percent). Adolescents using progesterone-only pills experienced a 120 percent higher rate of depression. While causation could not be clearly proved in such a study, the researchers found it difficult to find a social or reverse-causation scenario, which could explain the levels of increased risk over so many ages and types of contraception. In an interview following the study's release, one of the lead investigators expressed her opinion that the evidence indicated causation. She pointed to the findings that depression was more associated with the drugs containing more synthetic hormone, and that the longer a woman had used the hormones, the more likely she was to use antidepressants. Further, the authors did not find any emotional or relationship factors which could account for such effects – across women of so many ages and methods and relationship circumstances – as well as their common use of hormonal contraception.

The study was greeted with relief by many women, who felt that it validated their experience with hormonal contraception. One essay, published in the British Broadcasting Corporation's news magazine,[98] captured some of the most common themes of women's reactions. The author, Vicky Spratt, speaks of the excitement of the "rite of passage" of receiving her first pill prescription: "I was a woman now. In the plastic pockets was the sugar-coated

[96] Elinda A. Pletzer and Hubert H. Kerschbaum, "Fifty years of hormonal contraception – time to find out, what it does to our brain," *Frontiers in Neuroscience* 8 (August 2014): 1–6.

[97] Charlotte Wessel Skovlund et al., "Association of Hormonal Contraception with Depression," *Journal of the American Medical Association, Psychiatry* 73 (2016): 1154–1162.

[98] Vicky Spratt, "My Nightmare on the Pill," *British Broadcasting Corporation News Magazine*, January 11, 2017, www.bbc.com/news/magazine-38575745?SThisFB.

distillation of feminism, of women's liberation, of medical innovation." Afterwards, for many years, she experienced severe panic attacks, depression and other mental disturbances, until she ceased taking any hormonal contraceptives. She felt vindicated by the new research.

The study's findings were downplayed on the website of the federal National Library of Medicine, where the public was reminded several times that causation was not proven,[99] despite the study's lead author having expressed the strong opinion that causation was the best explanation.

Civil Rights

A portion of the resistance to federal contraception programs is linked to suspicion of government within minority communities. According to a sizable literature, black and Latina women worry more about the safety and side effects of contraception and are more apt to wonder about conspiracies to limit their family size. Some studies and anecdotal reports assert that black or Latina women have also felt pressured to start contraception, to be sterilized, or to use a method they did not prefer.[100] Beginning with the controversies in the 1970s – when the National Association for the Advancement of Colored People (NAACP) chapter first called contraceptive programs "Black Genocide" – to today, the theme of minority pressure refuses to disappear.[101] Governmental programs in the 1990s offering money to poor, minority women to use long-acting contraceptives, kept suspicion alive.[102] Government's significant efforts to make contraception and abortion available in minority communities also encounter greater pregnancy ambivalence and a more positive orientation toward younger motherhood in those same communities.[103] Leading contraception advocate the Guttmacher Institute has written[104] about how to promote contraception access in minority communities, while guarding against coercion and perceptions of coercion.

---

[99] US National Library of Medicine, "Women taking the contraceptive pill 'more likely to be depressed'," PubMedHealth, September 30, 2016, www.ncbi.nlm.nih.gov/pubmedhealth/behindtheheadlines/news/2016-09-30-women-taking-the-contraceptive-pill-more-likely-to-be-depressed/.

[100] See, e.g., Sheryl Thorburn Bird and Laura M. Bogart, "Birth Control Conspiracy Beliefs, Perceived Discrimination, and Contraception among African Americans: An Exploratory Study," *Journal of Health Psychology* 8 (2003): 263–276.

[101] Life Dynamics, Maafa21, Black Genocide in 21st Century America, www.maafa21.com/.

[102] Dorothy E. Roberts, *Killing the Black Body: Race, Reproduction and the Meaning of Liberty* (New York: Vintage, 1998), 104–117.

[103] Rachel Benson Gold, "Guarding Against Coercion While Insuring Access: A Delicate Balance," *The Guttmacher Policy Review*, September 2, 2014, www.guttmacher.org/gpr/2014/09/guarding-against-coercion-while-ensuring-access-delicate-balance.

[104] Ibid.

In addition to concerns about their health and freedom from governmental control, poor women – who experience the highest rates of unintended and nonmarital pregnancy – tell researchers in qualitative studies that their decisions about contraception are not governed by cost or availability. Rather, they are familiar with local providers, many of whom offer contraception free or at very low cost. According to the interviews in *Promises I Can Keep*, their decisions are based more upon factors such as the status of their relationship with a man; their desire for a child even while unmarried; their future plans, and the man's desire to have sex without contraception. In other words, it is not a straightforward matter of knowledge about contraception, or its supply, or its cost, which drives its usage.[105]

Risk Compensation?

The failure of the government's efforts to reduce unintended pregnancy may also have been due to a phenomenon called "risk compensation." It has generated a substantial literature,[106] and finds support even from doctors associated with contraception advocate, the Guttmacher Institute.[107] In the most well-known paper on this subject – "An Analysis of Out-of-Wedlock Childbearing in the United States" – Nobel prize-winning economist George A. Akerlof, Federal Reserve Chair Janet Yellen, and economist David Katz explain women's increased participation in nonmarital sexual relations following the increased availability and legalization of both contraception and abortion.

The authors claim that, as compared with other explanations of nonmarital pregnancies and birth, their "technology shock" hypothesis – combined with the declining stigma of a nonmarital birth – better explains the magnitude and timing of changes in the numbers and rates of nonmarital pregnancies and births during a historical period in which federal, state and private support and funding for contraception were increasing.

[105] Kathryn Edin and Maria J. Kefalas, *Promises I Can Keep: Why Poor Women Put Motherhood Before Marriage* (Berkeley: University of California Press, 2011), 34–47.

[106] See George A. Akerlof et al., "An Analysis of Out-of-Wedlock Childbearing in the United States," *The Quarterly Journal of Economics*; David Paton, "The Economics of Family Planning and Underage Conceptions," *Journal of Health Economics* 21 (2002): 27; Peter Arcidiacono et al., "Habit Persistence and Teen Sex: Could Increased Access to Contraception Have Unintended Consequences for Teen Pregnancies?" *Journal of Business and Economic Statistics* 30 (2012): 312.

[107] Lawrence B. Finer, "Trends in Premarital Sex in the United States: 1954–2003," *Public Health Reports* 122 (2007): 73; John S. Santelli and Andrea J. Melnikas, "Teen Fertility in Transition: Recent and Historic Trends in the United States," *Annual Review of Public Health* 31 (2010): 371–83.

They conclude that the current sex and mating market, enabled by contraception and abortion, operates to the disadvantage of women respecting pregnancy and marriage, and the relative advantage of men, due to a series of incentives structured by their availability. First, "[w]hen the cost of abortion is low, or contraceptives are readily available, potential male partners can easily obtain sexual satisfaction without making ... promises [to marry in the event of pregnancy] and will thus be reluctant to commit to marriage." Single women thus feel "pressured," because if they do not participate in sex, they are at a classic "competitive disadvantage" because"[s]exual activity without commitment is increasingly expected in premarital relationships." "If they ask for ... a guarantee [of marriage in the event of pregnancy], they are afraid that their partners will seek other relationships." The stigma of nonmarital parenting then declines as more and more women bear children without marriage.[108]

According to this theory, even women who want children, reject contraception and abortion, and want a marriage guarantee as a condition for sex, have nonmarital sex anyway because it is the price of entering the mating market. Such a market, in these researchers' view, is therefore likely to produce higher rates of sexual activity, nonmarital pregnancy, nonmarital birth and abortion all at the same time.

Sociologist Sara McLanahan, relying upon the Akerlof, Yellen and Katz research, notes that, while the pill likely boosted women's confidence to invest in advanced education, it is also true that both the pill and legalized abortion made it "easier for men to shirk their parental responsibilities."[109]

The evidence of risk compensation is not conclusive, but has significant support. Some authors reject the application of economic rationales to women or to the sexual marketplace, and caricature the theory in order to overcome it. One reporter, for example, claims that the theory proposes that "as soon as oral contraception came on the scene ..., horny females starting jumping into bed with anyone with a Y chromosome."[110] Despite such mischaracterizations, the theory enjoys widespread academic support.

Furthermore, frequent qualitative and anecdotal support comes from the multiplication of women's stories in books surveying "hookup culture" on college campuses. Regularly, women there report that sex has become

---

[108] Akerlof et al., "An Analysis of Out-of-Wedlock Childbearing in the United States," 280, 290, 296, 305.

[109] Sara McLanahan, "Diverging Destinies: How Children are Faring Under the Second Demographic Transition," *Demography* 41, no. 4 (2004): 618.

[110] Christina Sterbenz, "The Economics of Sex Theory Is Completely Wrong," *Business Insider*, March 3, 2014, www.businessinsider.com/economics-of-sex-video-debunked-2014-2.

the "price" of entering into a romantic relationship. This literature will be considered further in Chapter Four.

The Move to LARCs

Within especially the last decade, there has emerged a groundswell of support for long acting reversible contraceptives (LARCs). LARCS are generally defined to include Intrauterine devices (IUDs) which can work for three to ten years; implants, which are inserted under the skin and release hormones for about three years; and sometimes Depo Provera, a hormonal shot administered every three months. More women are using them than even ten or fifteen years ago. The case for LARCs' preventing unintended pregnancies appears fairly strong. They work over an extended period of time, and have superior effectiveness rates, as compared especially with forms of contraception that require daily or weekly attention. For those who err in their use of contraception, or who forget to ingest or apply it, or who are very young and irregular in their habits, or who are ambivalent about pregnancy – LARCs seem to be a superior method of preventing pregnancy. Often supporters cite the "cost effectiveness" of LARCs – that is, their ability to reduce public welfare expenditures for children.[111]

LARCs supporters are influential, together and apart. They include interest groups such as Planned Parenthood, the Guttmacher Institute, NCTUP, and influential think tanks such as the Brookings Institution[112] and the RAND Corporation.[113] Importantly, they also include medical associations, including The American College of Obstetricians and Gynecologists, which recommends offering women LARCs immediately post-delivery and has called them a "first line" choice.[114]

---

[111] See, e.g., Priya Batra and Chloe E. Bird, "Policy Barriers to Best Practices: The Impact of Restrictive State Regulations on Access to Long-Acting Reversible Contraceptives," The Rand Blog, November 6, 2015, at www.rand.org/blog/2015/11/policy-barriers-to-best-practices-the-impact-of-restrictive.html. ("[E]ach dollar spent on LARC methods yields a $5 return on investment in public insurance expenditures for unintended births.")

[112] Eleanor Krause and Isabel V. Sawhill, "Low-maintenance birth control: Gaining popularity, but barriers remain," Brookings: Social Mobility Memos, December 7, 2016, www.brookings.edu/blog/social-mobility-memos/2016/12/07/low-maintenance-birth-control-gaining-popularity-but-barriers-remain//.

[113] Batra and Bird, "Policy Barriers to Best Practices: The Impact of Restrictive State Regulations on Access to Long-Acting Reversible Contraceptives."

[114] American College of Obstetricians and Gynecologists, Committee Opinion Summary, No. 670, August 2016; see also www.acog.org/Patients/FAQs/Long-Acting-Reversible-Contraception-LARC-IUD-and-Implant.

The federal government, too, has demonstrated its hopes that LARCs will accomplish what its long existing contraception programs have failed to do. It usually begins its case for LARCS by acknowledging that the last fifty years' birth control efforts have been a great disappointment. It regularly today characterizes the range of contraceptives offered to American women and girls for the last half-century as less effective, while branding only LARCs and sterilization "most effective."[115]

A significant element of the ACA's contraception mandate was its hoped-for effect to make LARCS more readily available. This point was stressed in the Institute of Medicine's recommendation to HHS to establish the mandate.[116]

As described in Chapter One, federal Medicaid authorities have recently intensified their efforts to deliver LARCs to poor women by reminding providers of the high reimbursement rate, and women's ability to seek LARCs out of network. They are also recommending to providers that they advance-stock LARCs, encourage Medicaid women to receive them immediately post-partum, and advise women throughout their prenatal care of the immediate post-partum availability of LARCS.

The federal government has also helped fund a trial of LARCs among predominantly young, minority and low-income women in St. Louis. Its outcome has been heralded as evidence of the necessity of boosting LARCs' role in public and private contraception programs, although criticisms of the program have also been sharp.

The St. Louis study[117] recruited over 9,000 women, ages fourteen to forty-five years, between 2007 and 2011. Thirty-seven percent were receiving public assistance; 51 percent were African American; 42 percent had had an abortion; 63 percent had had a prior unintended pregnancy; and 35 percent possessed a high school degree or less. Participants recruited at abortion clinics were more likely to report a history of three or more unintended pregnancies. Participants were encouraged to switch to hormonal implants or IUDs at no cost.

Although at the time only 5 percent of women nationally used LARCs, 75 percent of program participants in the St. Louis study ultimately adopted

---

[115] US Centers for Disease Control, "Update: Providing Quality Family Planning Services – Recommendations from CDC and the U.S. Office of Population Affairs, 2015," Loretta Gavin and Karen Pazol, US Centers for Disease Control, *Morbidity and Mortality Weekly Report* 65 (March 11, 2016): 231–234; and, US Centers for Disease Control, "How Effective are Birth Control Methods?," at www.cdc.gov/reproductivehealth/contraception/.

[116] Institute of Medicine, *Clinical Preventive Services for Women*, 108.

[117] Jeffery Peipert et al. "Preventing Unintended Pregnancies by Providing No-Cost Contraception," *Journal of Obstetrics and Gynecology* 120 (2010): 1291–1297.

LARCs. Researchers contacted the patients seven times over the first three years of use in order to monitor and encourage continuation. After three years, rates of pregnancies and abortions declined significantly. The study claimed that abortion rates in were reduced to less than half of the national and regional rates among participants.

The study was widely praised by the American College of Obstetricians and Gynecologists and the *New York Times*, which reported that "free birth control led to greatly lower rates of abortions and births to teenagers, a large study concludes, offering strong evidence for how a bitterly contested Obama administration policy could benefit women's health."[118]

Scholars and journalists, however, questioned its results. They noted that, while St. Louis' teen abortion rates were lower than sexually-active teens nationally, the likelihood that a pregnancy ended in abortion was three times the national average; the national "abortion ratio" (abortions per 1,000 live births) among 15 to 19 year olds was about 33 percent at the time, but participants in the St. Louis study aborted nearly 100 percent of their pregnancies.[119] The study was also critiqued for its lack of a control group, and for its high percentage of post-aborted participants, who would have an unusually strong interest in avoiding pregnancy and a repeat abortion. The study was also faulted for its failure to measure how the program impacted sexual activity – that is, its association with numbers of sexual partners and interactions, and the status of the partners' relationships. It also failed to measure any incidence of STIs, depression, or other health effects.[120]

At the end of the three-year study (2010), the Center for Disease Control reported a 46 percent jump in syphilis, a 31 percent rise in gonorrhea and a 3 percent increase in chlamydia in St. Louis.[121] Supporters of the Choice project wrote off the increase as an artifact of stepped-up STIs reporting. But a 2015 study generated significant concern that, especially among teens,

---

[118] The Associated Press, "Study Finds Free Contraceptives Cut Abortion Rate," The *New York Times*, October 4, 2012, www.nytimes.com/2012/10/05/us/study-finds-free-contraceptives-cut-abortion-rate.html?_r=0.

[119] See US Centers for Disease Control, "Abortion Surveillance, United States, 2011," by Karen Pazol, et al., U. S. Centers for Disease Control, *Morbidity and Mortality Weekly Report*, November 28, 2014/63 (SS11); 1–41, TABLE 2. Number, rate, and ratio of reported abortions, by reporting area of residence and occurrence and by percentage of abortions obtained by out-of-state residents – United States, 2011, www.cdc.gov/mmwr/preview/mmwrhtml/ss6311a1.htm#Tab2.

[120] Michael New, "Study Exaggerates Benefits of No-Cost Contraception," The *National Review*, October 10, 2012, www.nationalreview.com/corner/329898/new-study-exaggerates-benefits-no-cost-contraception-michael-j-new.

[121] US Centers for Disease Control, *Sexually Transmitted Disease Surveillance 2010*, 93–95, 113, 119–20, 127, 129 (2011), www.cdc/gov/std/stats10/surv2010.pdf.

LARCs may promote or at least correlate with higher rates of STIs. It found that teens using LARCs were 60 percent less likely to use condoms, than those using oral contraceptives. Researchers further wrote that they remained unsure whether teens with more partners tend to be counseled to use LARCs or whether LARCs provoked more sexual partners; but they found that LARCs users were more than twice as likely to have two or more partners in the last three months, and twice as likely to have four or more lifetime partners, than women who did not use LARCs.[122]

The St. Louis study was further critiqued because the repeat abortion rate in St Louis declined only from 48 to 46 percent – a small amount – and was measured only by the decline in abortions at one clinic, although there were other abortion clinics in the St. Louis area. Given the relatively low take-up rate of LARCs nationally, critics also wondered if study results could be replicated with women who were not poor, post-aborted, and disadvantaged.

Another LARCs promotion trial was conducted in Colorado in 2009, but used state and private, not federal, funds. Still it was heralded by the same group of nationally influential LARCs supporters, and by representatives or grantees of the federal government. In this trial, researchers provided low-income women and teens free or low-cost LARCs. Researchers credited the program with driving down the rates of abortions and teen births.

Critics noted, however,[123] that it was difficult to disentangle program effects from dramatic reductions in Colorado's abortion rate prior to the program's initiation. Counties with the program experienced a 34 percent decline, while counties without it experienced a 29 percent decline. In reporting their results, researchers compared whole counties where women did not get the program with whole counties in which tiny subsections of women had accessed the program; yet they attributed the overall decline in the latter counties to the program.

[122] Riley J. Steiner et al., "Long-Acting Reversible Contraception and Condom Use Among Female US High School Students: Implications for Sexually Transmitted Infection Prevention," *Journal of the American Medical Association Pediatrics* 170 (2016); see also Julia Potter and Karen Soren, "Long-Acting Reversible Contraception and Condom Use: We Need a Better Message," *Journal of the American Medical Association Pediatrics* 170 (2016): 417–418.

[123] Callie Gable, "No, One Program Did Not Reduce Colorado's Teen Pregnancy Rate by 40 Percent," *National Review*, August 25, 2014, www.nationalreview.com/agenda/385884/no-one-program-did-not-reduce-colorados-teen-pregnancy-rate-40-percent-callie-gable; Megan McArdle, "Free Contraception Can't End the Abortion Debate," *Bloomberg View* (National), August 7, 2015, www.bloomberg.com/view/articles/2015-08-07/free-contraception-can-t-end-the-abortion-debate.

Regarding teen birth rates: for purposes of calculating program effects, researchers assumed that low-income teen pregnancy rates would continue unchanged from their numbers at the beginning of the program; they consequently attributed any declines to the program. Teen birth rates, however, were declining, statewide and nationally, even before the program began. Also, given that only 8,400 of 420,000 teens living in the state of Colorado received LARCs under the program, it appeared that the program could not be deemed responsible for much, let alone most, of the drop in the entire state's teen birth rates.

It remains unknown whether the St. Louis or Colorado models could be scaled up or repeated, given what is known about women's rates of discontinuation especially of hormonal birth control, and its health effects, and also given that more advantaged women eschew LARCs more often.[124] According to a 2015 summary of federal family planning efforts, commissioned by the government, however, stepped up endorsement of LARCS is having some effect. More women nationally are using LARCS in 2015 (15 percent) than in 2001 (4 percent).[125] Higher income women use LARCs at lower rates than lower-income women.

LARCs do not have unqualified support.[126] They continue to raise questions about women's health. Critics remain concerned about social effects; especially risk compensation, and racial and socio-economic targeting. Furthermore, they can only be administered by medical personnel, and only medical personnel can remove them. Supporters sometimes refer to them as "free of user control" or "independent of user motivation."[127] Qualms are stronger in minority and poor communities.[128] These and other ethical questions will be treated at greater length in Chapter Four.

---

[124] US Department of Health and Human Services, *Family Planning Annual Report: 2015 National Summary*, by Christina Fowler, et al., U.S. Department of Health and Human Services (Research Triangle Park: RTI International, 2016), www.hhs.gov/opa/sites/default/files/title-x-fpar-2015.pdf.

[125] Ibid.

[126] See, e.g., The American Enterprise Institute and the Brookings Institution Working Group on Poverty and Opportunity, *Opportunity, Responsibility, and Security: A Consensus Plan for Reducing Poverty and Restoring the American Dream* (Washington, DC: The American Enterprise Institute for Public Policy Research and the Brookings Institution, 2015), https://www.brookings.edu/wp-content/uploads/2016/07/Full-Report.pdf, 36.

[127] Laura Bassett, "Access To Free Birth Control Causes Abortion Rate to Drop Dramatically: Study," *The Huffington Post*, October 5, 2012, www.huffingtonpost.com/2012/10/05/study-free-birth-control-abortion-rate_n_1942621.html.

[128] Jenny A. Higgins, "Celebration Meets Cautions, LARC's Boons, Potential Busts and the Benefits of a Reproductive Justice Approach," *Contraception* 89 (2014): 237–241.

SUMMARY AND CONCLUSION: CONTRACEPTION

So far, federal contraception programs for adults have not succeeded, even on the federal government's own terms: reducing unintended pregnancy. It appears that a variety of factors account for women's less than wholehearted response to contraception. Health and side effects account for some resistance, including preexisting health conditions contraindicating for hormonal contraception. Poorer women's relationship circumstances, and the low opportunity costs of their having a child, are also factors. Risk compensation also appears to play a role.

LARCs are gaining in popularity, and recent studies provide some reason to believe that they might reduce unintended pregnancies. At the same time, these studies are not without significant flaws, and may not be generalizable to the population of women in the United States. As I will suggest in the next chapter, there may also be ethical problems, which could counsel against the federal government's continuing to promote contraception in the same manner as it has in the past. Assuming, as I do, that these programs will continue, there is very likely a better, more responsible way to speak to women and men concerning contraception.

4

An Ethical and Anthropological Critique

At first glance, both sexual expressionism and the federal responses to the situation of nonmarital children seem inevitable: the only possible responses in contemporary times. Contraception altered the sex and marriage markets. Technology and the economy changed opportunities and possibilities for employment and marriage. Public opinions regarding nonmarital sex and new family structures shifted considerably.

A closer look, however, reveals more than a few important defects in this account. For, even accepting the most generous interpretation of federal rationales for adopting sexual expressionism, it is clear today, not only that the government relied upon a flawed understanding of human nature – a flawed "anthropology" – but also that it crossed ethical lines. It ignored obligations to children, both directly, and by means of undercutting their parent's stability. It proposed responses which either repeated these mistakes, or were insufficient to the point of being unethical.

This chapter will first address the ethical and anthropological failings of sexual expressionism itself, and then critique the government's "back door" and contraception responses to the consequent difficulties faced by children.

THE PROBLEMS OF SEXUAL EXPRESSIONISM

Before turning to the substantive ethical problems posed by sexual expressionism, it is important to note a quantitative aspect. Children are everyone, every single human being, and for a crucial portion of every lifetime. Their wellbeing is, by definition, our wellbeing – each family's, each school's, each community's, each employer's and the nation's as a whole. While the numbers of persons affected by a policy may not substantively exacerbate its ethical problems, quantitatively, it matters.

Children's Vulnerability and the Corresponding Obligation

There is a great deal of intuitive and scholarly support for the idea that more vulnerable human beings are owed a duty of care from the more powerful. That adults bring their children into being further strengthens this obligation. I will treat this second aspect after the first.

Philosopher Hans Jonas – widely credited with valorizing the notion of human responsibility for the natural environment and for future generations – succinctly communicates adults' obligation to children in his book *The Imperative of Responsibility*:

> For when asked for a single instance … where that coincidence of "is" and "ought" occurs, we can point at the most familiar sight: the newborn, whose mere breathing uncontradictably addresses an ought to the world around, namely to take care of him.[1]

Jonas proposes that the child is the "archetypal" example of a demand for timely responsibility. The child is both a living person and "not yet." The child requires help securing her proper ends. Jonas refers to the "radical insufficiency" of "the begotten," and the "pledge thereto" as "implicit in the act of generation." He argues further that omission is "as lethal as commission" where the child's well-being and ends are concerned.[2]

Others have reached similar conclusions. Law professor Greg Loken writes that duties to infants "have a virtually self-evident quality based on the newborn's utter neediness."[3] Philosopher Cynthia Willett grounds adult responsibility in part upon the vast differences in adults' and children's relative power, and the "unearned privilege" of being older.[4]

Willett also makes an appealing and important case for what justice requires of adults beginning at conception, based upon a more child-aware reading of John Rawls' *A Theory of Justice*.[5] Rawls' analysis highlights the rights of an individual who is making choices from "behind the veil of ignorance" regarding

---

[1] Hans Jonas, *The Imperative of Responsibility: In Search of an Ethics for the Technological Age* (Chicago: The University of Chicago Press, 1984), 131.

[2] Id., 134–135.

[3] Gregory A. Loken, "Gratitude and the Map of Moral Duties Toward Children," *Arizona. State Law Journal* 31 (1999): 1121, 1129.

[4] See Cynthia Willett, "Collective Responsibility for Children in an Age of Orphans," in *The Best Love of the Child: Being Loved and Being Taught to Love as the First Human Right*, ed. Timothy P. Jackson (Grand Rapids: William B. Eerdmans Publishing Company, 2011): 179–196, 194.

[5] John Rawls, *A Theory of Justice*, Rev. Ed. (Cambridge: Belknap Press of Harvard University, 1999), 118–123.

his personal and social circumstances. Willett proposes that this is an inadequate framework for considering justice to children. Their earliest family circumstances are entirely dependent upon the adults in their lives. An adequate analysis would therefore have to take account of what the adult owes the child. Willett argues, in fact, that the only ethical method adequate to children "that would claim the force of universality ... or otherwise some binding force over another, is the statement of that demand from the language and perspective of the disempowered Other."[6] Further addressing Rawls, she concludes that he understood liberty insufficiently: in negative terms, as the ability to make choices. This is not sufficient where there is vulnerability, because the vulnerable require solidarity for justice. Willett surmises that Rawls' view likely derives from strong currents in Anglo-Saxon liberal theory viewing external authority or unchosen meaning as the opposite of autonomy.[7] She insists, rightly, that this must not apply to children.

Willett finds philosopher Martha Nussbaum's capability theory of justice more adequate than Rawls' theory, but still unrealistic and likely ineffective.[8] Nussbaum proposes that a correct theory of justice involves capacitating persons to achieve minimal functioning respecting certain identified capabilities. Willet acknowledges that Nussbaum better accounts for human beings' intrinsically social nature, but faults her for leaving the work of helping the most dependent to the mercy of persons' moral sympathies or to their altruism. According to Willett, justice for children requires more because it is very difficult to persuade people to care about other people's children. Moral sympathy is insufficient. Willett rightly points out that only the hard work of negotiation, reparation and compromise can forward children's interests.[9]

Certainly, these are not new thoughts or projects in U.S. family law, which recognizes parents' duties to children in the laws governing support, abuse and neglect. Family law scholars also regularly advocate for positive duties toward children. Influential family scholar Martha Fineman[10] has written, for example, that the vulnerable subject should replace the autonomous subject within family law due to the inevitability of dependency and humans'

---

6 Cynthia Willett, *Maternal Ethics and Other Slave Moralities* (New York: Routledge, 1995), 4.
7 Cynthia Willett, "Collective Responsibility for Children in an Age of Orphans," 180–183.
8 *Id.*, 183–187, discussing Martha Nussbaum, *Frontiers of Justice: Disability, Nationality, Species Membership* (Cambridge: The Belknap Press of Harvard University, 2006).
9 *Id.*, 189–190, 194.
10 See, e.g., Martha Albertson Fineman, "The Vulnerable Subject: Anchoring Equality in the Human Condition," *Yale Journal of Law and Feminism* 20 (2008): 1–23; and Martha Fineman, "Masking Dependency: The Political Role of Family Rhetoric," *Virginia Law Review* 81 (1995): 2181.

embeddedness in webs of relations. She reasons that this new framework should result in strengthened governmental obligations to vulnerable subjects.

Judging from a few recent U.S. family law proposals, there appears to be growing support for strengthening parental responsibility to children by going further "back in time" and further beyond tangible support. Law professor Shari Motro, for example has recommended requiring fathers to pay "preg-limony," to the mothers of their children during the entire pregnancy.[11] Law professor Merle Weiner has proposed strengthening unmarried biological parents' joint responsibility to their common child, by increasing the partners' responsibility to cooperate with one another, even to perform "relationship work" for the child's benefit.[12]

Given that a child's family structure is largely established at conception, and given the relationship between family structure and child welfare, a proper and realistic set of ethical guidelines for adults includes taking responsibility for a child's family structure beginning at conception. This promotes parental stability, which is so important for capacitating children. This empowers children's open future. This helps to avoid relying upon the moral sympathies and altruism of strangers, and the unevenness and incompleteness of bureaucratic remedies. At the very least, the state should promote and assist marital parenting, and not ignore or undermine it.

A note here about how governmental promotion of a child's well-being from conception might work in the context of our constitutional right of legal abortion. A consistently pro-child stance would include solidarity by the state with unborn as well as born children. This would help avoid the situation we face today, in which abortion is legal for any reason, yet institutions and individuals are strenuously urged to care for children with both public and private resources from the moment the mother is pregnant.

Assuming the continuation of widely legal abortion, however, it remains possible for the state to be solicitous regarding children's family structure at conception, on the grounds of the duty of care for every child brought to birth. This is not to understate the intellectual and practical challenges that legal abortion poses to this outcome. Legal abortion communicates that those who are most dependent upon adults are precisely those whom adults have a legal right to kill. It communicates further that adults can legally kill *only* their own children. On the one hand, it seems impossible to cordon off this part of family law from other parts. On the other hand, it remains possible to say that

---

[11] Shari Motro, "The Price of Pleasure," *Northwestern University Law Review* 104 (2010): 917.

[12] Merle Weiner, *A Parent–Partner Status for American Family Law* (Cambridge: Cambridge University Press, 2015).

there is nothing stopping the state from speaking strongly in favor of adults' assuming responsibility for children who are conceived and born and recognized as citizens and neighbors – even against the backdrop of legal abortion.

Knowledge Implies Responsibility

As Chapter Two stated, we know today that, on average, children benefit substantially from the stable care of both parents. We know that stable and continuous care is most likely to be achieved within marriage, even if other relationships may sometimes provide it. Married, biological parents possess a unique set of inclinations and opportunities relative to their own children.

Hans Jonas observes that parents owe more than the basics (food, clothing, shelter) to their children, because these alone will not capacitate a child to be what he or she needs to be. Parents are rather responsible for the child "as a whole" including – to the extent parents' can influence these – the child's character, knowledge, happiness, and socialization.[13]

Parents' obligations to their children may be even more extensive today, given what is known about the likely complexity, fluidity, and global interdependence of a future economy. Children will need significant education or training. They will also require significant emotional intelligence.

These ethical propositions already enjoy some support in U.S. family law. Children's rights scholars agree that children need continuity of care, and parental supports beyond basic needs.[14] Federal back door programs are based upon the same principle. Several of these programs work to enhance parenting skills such as encouragement, discipline, and responsiveness. This principle, however, has not yet been applied prenatally, to the time of conception, and to the matter of the formation of children's family structure.

We Make Them

Sexual expressionism likewise contradicts adults' responsibilities for human lives they have caused to exist: it insufficiently attends to the circumstances of children's birth, and to the good of the parents' stable union.

Hans Jonas again speaks incisively to the relevant ethical principle. He writes that "causing" involves responsibility for what we cause, because when

---

[13] Jonas, *The Imperative of Responsibility*, 101–102.
[14] See, e.g., Anne L. Alstott, *No Exit: What Parents Owe Their Children and What Societies Owes Parents* (Oxford: Oxford University Press, 2004), 33–36; and Richard Weissbourd, *The Vulnerable Child: What Really Hurts America's Children and What We Can Do About It* (Reading, Massachusetts: Addison-Wesley Publishing Company, 1996), 8.

the "effects of our deeds move into the future, our responsibility moves there too." That responsibility is a "correlate of power and must be commensurate with the latter's scope and that of its exercise."[15]

We know that adult deeds – conceiving children under particular circumstances – meaningfully affect children's future. Commensurate responsibility is therefore due at that moment. This call to responsibility is all the more urgent because of the human tendency to valorize or normalize the demands and desires of the present moment. Jonas nearly perfectly captures the problematic situation obtaining at the moment of conception when he observes that, "only *present* interests make themselves heard and felt and enforce their consideration.... But the *future* is not represented. It is not a force that can throw its weight into the scales. The nonexistent has no lobby, and the unborn are powerless."[16]

Already, family law automatically assigns biological parents responsibility for their children. Parents who cause children to exist by means of assisted reproductive technologies are regularly treated similarly. Courts rebuff biological fathers' attempts to evade child support obligations on the grounds that a sexual partner assured him that she was using birth control, or would absolve him of support obligations. Because he helped to cause the child, his responsibility rather continues until the child is an adult, or is legally removed from the parents' care. A reversal of federal sexual expressionism is therefore in sync with family law's ethical default practice of assigning responsibility to the adults who make a child. It would simply requires extending responsibility back in time, to the important moment when the child's family structure hangs in the balance.

Sexual Expressionism Weakens the Parental Relationship on Which Children Depend

Undercutting Parents' Stability

Children benefit from their parents' synergies, in addition to what each parent provides uniquely and additively. A pro-child policy would therefore assist the stability of parents' unions. Sexual expressionism, however, with its focus on individual sexual desires and its frequent indifference to marriage, undercuts partner stability. It does so by separating out the idea of children from sexual intercourse.

---

[15] Jonas, *The Imperative of Responsibility*, x.
[16] Id., 22. (emphasis original).

Philosopher Zygmunt Bauman – creator of the notions of "liquid love" and "liquid modernity" – rightly observes that this separation of children from sex effectively also separates both sex and children from the concepts of love, kin, family, union, and future, and places children rather under the umbrellas of "consumption" and "pleasure."[17]

Sociologist Anthony Giddens comes to similar conclusions by a different analysis. He shows that excising the idea of children from sex transforms sex, narrowing the entire focus to the male/female relation. This gives rise to what Giddens terms the "pure relationship" wherein continuity is determined solely by each person's evaluation of his or her own satisfaction for so long as it may last.[18] This has no point of intersection with a child's need for the steady assistance of these two adults. Giddens further and rightly predicted that in this environment, marriage changes meaning. It becomes a "shell" retaining the same name as the former institution, but holding new contents.[19] It is no longer necessarily committed, or attuned to or integrated with children. Children are a decision apart from the individual spouses' decision to love one another, and even apart from their marriage.[20]

Philosopher Charles Taylor sees the unlinking of sex and children as an extension of utilitarianism into the relational arena. With the excising of children from sex, and the ability of sex to deliver pleasure, sex begins to center more upon the utility of my body, as "matter" to be used for my purposes. This easily leads to a great deal of "mobility" in relationships, which puts at risk everything that depends upon stable personal relationships: kin, marriage and even the polity. Taylor also links this form of utilitarianism, and the weak associations it encourages, to adults' surrendering self-governance. They can no longer rely upon their own family life as insurance, nor can their children. Thus arises the need for much more assistance from the state for nonmarital and other less stable households.[21]

Moving beyond the philosophical, several authors highlight the practical relationship between uncommitted sex and future couple stability. Sociologists

---

[17] Zygmunt Bauman, *Liquid Love* (Cambridge: Polity Press, 2003), 42–43, 47.

[18] Anthony Giddens, *The Transformation of Intimacy: Sexuality, Love, and Eroticism in Modern Societies* (Stanford: Stanford University Press, 1993), 2, 58.

[19] Id., 58, 135, 154.

[20] Anthony Giddens, "The Global Revolution in Family and Personal Life," in *Family in Transition*, ed. Arlene S. Skolnik and Jerome H. Skolnik (Boston: Pearson Education, Inc., 2009): 25–31, 29.

[21] Charles Taylor, *Sources of the Self: The Making of the Modern Identity* (Cambridge: Harvard University Press, 1989), 502–507.

Scott Stanley and Galena Rhoades, for example, in their paper *Before "I Do:" What do Premarital Experiences Have to Do With Marital Quality Among Today's Young Adults?*[22] chronicle the effects of couples deciding to pursue sex before they have a well-developed knowledge of one another. Couples intending commitment, as distinguished from those who "slide" into sex or cohabitation, or even marriage, have superior happiness and marital stability. Those with more premarital sexual partners often, though not in every case, experience lower marital quality and stability. Neurologists, too, observe that the human libido can be easily altered by our psychology and the history of our sexual encounters. Neurologist Norman Doidge, for example in his book *The Brain that Changes Itself*, observes: "[s]exual taste is obviously influenced by culture and experience and is often acquired and then wired into the brain. Behaviors influence our brain. Our choices have neurobiological effects"[23] Researchers Joe McIlhaney, Jr. and Freda McKissic Bush point out that human bodies' hormonal responses to sex – the dopamine reward, the oxytocin or vasopressin release – shape our desires and memories of sex for future sexual encounters. Additionally, with each sexual partner, it is possible that "synapses that govern decisions about sex in both the male and female brains are strengthened in ways that make it easier to choose to have sex in the future, while synapses that govern sexual restraint are weakened and deteriorate."[24]

Repeatedly in the "college-hookup" genre books, authors report young women's, and sometimes young men's, sense that early sex interfered with a relationship. They point out that, after beginning a sexual relationship it is harder to come to know one another through ordinary communications – talking casually or learning each other's opinions. They worry, too, that ordinary communications will afterwards seem boring. Rhoades and Stanley report similar findings in their study *Before "I Do."*

Disconnecting sex from even the idea of children, seems a wrongheaded approach to helping citizens eventually assume adult responsibilities toward children. The transition to parenthood involves coming to experience a romantic partner as a possible father or mother to a common child, whose welfare will be most parents' preeminent concern. In short, it involves learning to

---

22   Galena K. Rhoades and Scot M. Stanley, *Before "I Do:" What Do Premarital Experiences Have to Do with Marital Quality Among Today's Young Adults?* (The National Marriage Project, University of Virginia, 2014), www.nationalmarriageproject.org/wordpress/wp-content/uploads/2014/08/NMP-BeforeIDoReport-Final.pdf.

23   Norman Doidge, *The Brain That Changes Itself: Stories of Personal Triumph from the Frontiers of Brain Science* (New York: Viking, 2007).

24   Joe S. McIlhaney, Jr. and Freda McKissic Bush, *Hooked: New Science on How Casual Sex is Affecting Our Children* (Chicago: Northfield Publishing, 2008).

associate sex with ongoing partnership and with children. Sexual expressionism ignores the association of sex with procreating children, and of sex with partner stability, and focuses instead only on the couple as a couple, or on the individual as a person consenting to, consuming or desiring sex. Bauman points out, in fact, that when sex sheds even its association with children, rather than liberating the couple, this "overload[s]" sex with "expectations beyond its capacity to deliver."[25] The couple is led away from thoughts of their relationship, present or future, and toward preoccupations with pleasure and performance. In sum, sexual expressionism and the behaviors it defends, or even promotes, would seem to decapacitate men and women for a durable relationship and for parenthood, not to capacitate them.

Scrambling Communications

Current surveys show that people have become sharply divided regarding the meaning of sex. Even a survey of religious youth in 2015 revealed "how little everyone agrees on when it comes to the purpose of sex." The author of the survey commented that "[t]here's never been a shortage of conversations and cultural imagination around sex, but this current lack of consensus points to a growing ambiguity and tension over its place in society and in the individual's life."[26]

Today, sex might mean one or more of the following: Intimacy? Fun? Physical Pleasure? Instinct? Future? Children? Potential marriage? Love? The majority opinions in *Lawrence* and *Obergefell* stated flatly that sex inevitably means an enduring relationship. Others insist that it means no more and no less than what the partners are thinking at that moment. Zygmunt Bauman proposes that, when bodies unify, this has its own message, which even the "clever" slogan "safe sex" cannot alter.[27]

Even between partners there might exist disagreement. Contemporary hook-up books illustrate this lavishly: women and men have different expectations and conclusions. Separating sex from children and from marriage, as sexual expressionism does, helps to cause these misunderstandings. But when children are rather allowed to be an element of sex – even intellectually associated with sex – the couple's future also becomes an element. Even considering the possibility of children raises the question of the durability of the

---

[25] Bauman, *Liquid Love*, 47.

[26] The Barna Group, "What Americans Believe About Sex," Releases in Culture and Media, January, 14, 2016, www.barna.org/research/culture-media/research-release/what-americans-believe-about-sex#.V5DDkCOAOko. (Evangelical Christian polling.)

[27] Bauman, *Liquid Love*, 50.

couple's relationship. Practically and legally, children link the couple. At the personal level, they raise the question, too, of the desirability of the sexual partner as a potential father or mother to one's own child. All of this narrows the possible meanings of sex, channeling it toward intimacy, future, kin and marriage, and away from instinct and consumption. There is a greater possibility for mutual understanding.

Even historian Steven Seidman – an admirer of the new personal and social possibilities offered by sexual expressionism – notes the potential for uncommitted sex to increase misunderstandings between partners about the meaning of any particular sexual encounter.[28] Likewise, sociologist Eva Illouz – who recognizes some positive values in contemporary sexual practices – faults the "cult of sexual experience" as "interfer[ing] with the capacity of men and women to forge intense, all-involving meaningful bonds which provide one with a knowledge of the kind of persons one cares about."[29]

The Poor Pay More

Sexual expressionist federal laws and policies, applied in a uniform manner to disparate groups, are resulting in greater hardships for the poor. Chapter Two described the disproportionate rate of nonmarital births among the poor, and its role in social stratification. Many authors have pointed out how diminished family stability among the poor is readily explained on the grounds of the different constraints and opportunity costs within poor communities.

No one illustrates these better than sociologists Kathryn Edin and Maria Kefalas in their personal and poignant account of single mothers in Philadelphia and Camden, *Promises I Can Keep: Why Poor Women Put Motherhood Before Marriage*.[30] Here, in their own words, poor women reveal their preference for childbearing at a younger age, as well as their understanding that marital childbearing is best. Like all women, poorer women have a better chance of becoming pregnant before or near the age of thirty. Unlike more privileged women, however, the poor have far fewer marriageable men in their communities, due to joblessness, crime and drugs. Within their communities, there is also a powerful narrative of success, which involves rearing

---

[28] Steven Seidman, *Romantic Longings: Love in America, 1830–1980* (New York: Routledge, 1993), 5.

[29] Illouz, *Love Hurts*, 246.

[30] Kathryn Edin and Maria Kefalas, *Promises I Can Keep: Why Poor Women Put Motherhood Before Marriage* (Oakland: University of California Press, 2005).

a child as a single mother. Many of the women have not been treated as a "gift" by a present or involved father. Many do not perceive a realistic hope of a college education or a desirable job. Their opportunity costs are low. A child represents the possibility of a meaningful future, in which they have the opportunity to be a gift to another.

These conditions obtain no matter how much attention and funding the state devotes to contraception or even abortion. Poor women may have more abortions per capita than wealthier women, but they have a lower abortion ratio: i.e., abortions per pregnancies. The women interviewed by Edin and Kefalas knew where to find birth control and abortion easily. They chose to have their children.

Consider further that the government is far more active in poorer communities – through health centers, youth development programs, public schools, jobs programs, and Medicaid providers – with the message that sex should be separated from the idea of children. Additionally, according to sociologist Annette Lareau, in her book *Unequal Childhoods*, poorer families do not feel as empowered to criticize public institutions and professionals because of the powers such institutions possess to scrutinize their lives, including their parenting.[31]

Finally, there is too stark a contrast between the way in which the government interacts with the better off and the poor, insofar as nonmarital births are concerned. For decades, poor women and teenagers have been on the receiving end of enormous government "solicitude" about having and using contraception. In recent years – especially with the contraception mandate – the federal government has more actively pursued cheap contraception for better-off women, but with noticeable political or electioneering aims versus social or anti-poverty aims.

A realistic assessment of the federal government's actions over the last half-century might conclude that the government is far less interested in channeling *all* children into stable family situations – rich and poor alike – than it is interested in dampening birthrates among those who "cannot afford" children: teens and the poor. It is almost as if the government has no "hope" of poorer women moving toward more marital childbearing, or of helping poorer children receive the advantages of a father, within the context of a marital household. As for women who are not poor? The government simply recommends that they make their own "reproductive life plans" to have or not to have a nonmarital birth, as they choose.

---

[31] Annette Lareau, *Unequal Childhoods, Class, Race and Family Life*, 2nd ed. (Berkeley: University of California Press, 2011), 217.

Children's Identity Interests

There is no clearly established U.S., or international, family law "right to know and be reared by one's biological parents." The issue is live, however, due to practices such as assisted reproductive technologies, same-sex marriage, international adoption, and high rates of incarceration of adults who are also parents. Nonmarital children, too, often experience very diminished contact or even separation from a parent, especially a father.[32]

The question of a child's right to "gain a continuity with the past and a complete and consistent biography"[33] is also globally debated. Some propose that the European Convention on Human Rights, the Universal Declaration of Human Rights or the United Nations' Convention on the Rights of the Child include a child's right to know and be cared for by both of his or her parents.[34]

Sexual expressionism tends to normalize the separation of children from their fathers, and conflict with emerging support for children's relationship with both biological parents, perhaps even as a part of their interest in their "identity." In fact, it might be said that the Supreme Court's claim that adults' interests in "identity" include a right to sexual expression conflicts directly with children's identity interests.

In the last several decades, U.S. family law has increasingly accommodated children's interest in association with both parents. Open adoption has grown, as well as joint custody. Federal and state child protection laws stressing family rehabilitation and reunification also sound this theme, as do state laws facilitating adoption by relatives over non-kin. There is also a growing sympathy with children's interests in knowing the adults who participated in their "collaborative reproduction," (i.e., by means of "donor" eggs or sperm or embryos) as news reports and online venues highlight the significant number of children seeking contact with their parents and relatives.[35] The Donor Sibling

---

[32] Paul Amato et al., "Changes in Nonresident Father-Child Contact from 1976 to 2002," *Family Relations* 58 (2009): 41–53; and Laura Tach, Ronald Mincy and Kathryn Edin, "Parenting as a 'Package Deal': Relationships, Fertility, and Nonresident Father Involvement among Unmarried Parents," *Demography* 47 (2010): 181.

[33] Margaret Somerville, "A simple answer to Quebec's simple adoption question," *The Globe and Mail*, October 13, 2009, www.theglobeandmail.com/opinion/a-simple-answer-to-quebecs-simple-adoption-question/article4288658.

[34] Richard J. Blauwhoff, *Foundational Facts, Relative Truths: A Comparative Law Study on Children's Right to Know Their Genetic Origins* (Cambridge: Intersentia, 2009).

[35] See, e.g., Joanna E. Scheib, Alice Ruby and Jean Benward, "Who Requests Their Sperm Donor's Identity? The first ten years information-releases to adults with open-identity donors," *Mental Health, Sexuality and Ethics* 107 (2017): 483–493 (In exploring the meaning of the genetic connection with the donor, by comparing similarities between themselves and their donor, they hoped for an expanded sense of their identity. This process of identity formation

Registry, with at least 50,000 members since the year 2000, has connected more than 13,000 relatives to one another. A 2017 study revealed donor-created children's strong inclination to contact their fathers as part of the process of their identity formation.[36] U.S. law is also sensitive to the family unification interests of children in communities historically subjected to violence and family separation, such as Native Americans and African Americans. I am suggesting that this sensitivity might be extended to children in chronically poor communities as well.

Our Supreme Court has never held explicitly that children have a "right to their identity," or to access to both of their parents, but it is clear from its cases, and from a wide variety of federal and state laws, that the loss of either parent is regarded as a tragedy to be avoided. The Court has not addressed this in its sexual expressionism opinions – not even in the same-sex marriage cases that have the greatest potential to normalize the separation of children from their biological families. It has raised this question as a matter of children's moral and legal rights, however, in other cases treating children's family connections.

In the "grandparents' rights" case of *Troxel v. Granville*, for example, Justice Stevens wrote that:

> [w]hile this Court has not yet had occasion to elucidate the nature of a child's liberty interests in preserving established familial or family-like bonds, … it seems to me extremely likely that, to the extent parents and families have fundamental liberty interests in preserving such intimate relationships, so, too, do children have these interests, and so, too, must their interests be balanced in the equation.[37]

In *Adoptive Couple v. Baby Girl*[38] Justice Sotomayor extended the moral and legal argument. She argued in her dissent for the "principle, recognized in our cases, that the biological bond between parent and child is meaningful." She continued with a review of both state custody and adoption laws, and federal cases pointing to the possible existence of a constitutional right for children. Following a lengthy summary of state custody and parentage laws, and laws respecting unmarried fathers, Justice Sotomayor characterized these rules as

seemed important for their sense of belonging ("I'm different from the rest of my family") and comfort with oneself ("to feel more connected to parts of me that I have questions about.")) Elizabeth Marquardt, *My Daddy's Name is Donor* (New York: Institute for American Values, 2010), and AnonymousUs.org (website for sharing stories of third party reproduction).

[36] See Tamar Lewin, "Sperm Banks Accused of Losing Samples and Lying About Donors," *The New York Times*, July 21, 2016, www.nyti.ms/2abBIPI.

[37] Troxel v. Granville, 530 U.S. 57, 88 (Stevens, J. dissenting).

[38] Adoptive Couple v. Baby Girl, 133 S. Ct. 2552, 2574 (2013) (Sotomayor, J. dissenting).

recognizing that "biological fathers have a valid interest in a relationship with their child. And children have a reciprocal interest in knowing their biological parents." She described a child's lost opportunity to know both of his or her parents as a "los[s] [that] cannot be measured." She characterized U.S. family law as reflecting the "understanding that the biological bond between a parent and a child is a strong foundation on which a stable and caring relationship may be built."[39] Justice Sotomayor's opinion is consistent with many of American family law's impulses about maintaining children's links with their biological parents when possible, or re-establishing them if they are attenuated or temporarily disrupted. It moves in a direction opposite to the normalization of parent/child separations that sexual expressionism facilitates.

Individualism Is Not a Family Value

In their book *Inside the Castle: Law and the Family in 20th Century America*,[40] family law professors Joanna Grossman and Lawrence Friedman remark how much the "social concept of 'the family' has moved in a single direction ... toward family as a cluster of individuals." Sexual expressionism blesses this idea even at the moment when a dependent child's family structure is initiated. In fact, however, family is a nest of interdependencies. And not for brief periods. While it is true that human beings are not young or elderly forever, a person may be incapacitated for his or her entire life. Furthermore, children are in need of formation for many years; and they depend on their parents' interdependent union especially during that time. They may also depend upon their extended family.

Furthermore, in order to receive the care needed when one is elderly or sick, any family member must rely upon margins of affection and good will, built up over many years and many interactions, not just a few. Familial interdependency is a fact of life therefore for a great deal of time, and not for very limited periods.

Four female scholars – family law scholars Martha Fineman[41] and Mary Ann Glendon,[42] and philosophers Eva Feder Kittay[43] and Cynthia Willett[44] – have all written about the interdependent family, with different aims in mind. Each makes proposals that could support my critique of sexual expressionism on the

---

[39] Id., 2582.
[40] Joanna L. Grossman and Lawrence M. Friedman, *Inside the Castle: Law and the Family in 20th Century America* (Princeton: Princeton University Press, 2011), 22.
[41] Fineman, "The Vulnerable Subject," and "Masking Dependency."
[42] Mary Ann Glendon, *The Transformation of Family Law* (Chicago: University of Chicago Press, 1989).
[43] Eva Feder Kittay, *Love's Labor: Essays on Women, Equality, and Dependency* (New York: Routledge, 1999).
[44] Willett, "Collective Responsibility for Children in an Age of Orphans."

grounds of its excessive individualism. Professor Fineman wishes to secure more public responsibility for children, women, and caretaking. Professor Glendon aims to rebalance family law toward a proper acknowledgment both of individual rights and family solidarity. Professor Feder Kittay highlights the vulnerability of caretakers, and their need for both private and public support beyond what individualistic theories of justice would prescribe. And Professor Willett highlights the inadequacy of the contemporary values of individual freedom, equality and tolerance when it comes to understanding intrafamilial dependencies, or to properly sustaining them,

All agree that individualism is an inadequate model of family life. All of their analyses would support my conclusion that sexual expressionism is practically and even morally insufficient because it fails to take public responsibility for caretakers and children; it fails to balance individual and family interests; and it fails to qualify contemporary individualistic values with obligations to the vulnerable. Their reasoning easily extends to the matter of the state's responsibility to promote responsible care for children at the time when their family structure is ordinarily established.

It Was Never the Bacchanalia They Imagined

Even were the federal voice attempting only to secure an interest in sexual satisfaction or health, sexual expressionism misses the mark by emphasizing ephemeral and individual satisfaction, as distinct from what Americans prefer: a "couple orientation" and a desire for commitment.

The best accepted measure of human sexual practice in the United States, *The Social Organization of Sexuality: Sexual Practices in the United States*, indicates that Americans are happiest with their sex lives on average, when they are highly committed to another person, and oriented to the other's happiness as well as their own. The mere "expression" or acting out of a sexual behavior, for purposes of enacting one's identity or experiencing freedom, and without reference to the stability and commitment of the partnership, doesn't capture this set of preferences.

Americans report a modest number of sexual partners over the course of a lifetime, and enjoy sex more when it is in the context of a longer commitment. Both of these conclusions were disputed actively for a period of time following the 1948 and 1953 issuance of the *Kinsey Reports*[45] and the 1976 release of

---

[45] Alfred C. Kinsey et al., *Sexual Behavior in the Human Male* (Philadelphia: W.B. Saunders, 1948), Alfred C. Kinsey et al., *Sexual Behavior of the Human Female* (Philadelphia, W.B. Saunders, 1953).

the *Hite Report*.[46] Both claimed that American men and women had stronger inclinations than was previously imagined toward multiple sexual partners and adultery. Both reports are judged unreliable today, and far inferior to *The Social Organization of Sexuality*. In a companion book of scholarship, University of Chicago sociologist Linda Waite calls the survey an "accurate scientific report of the broad outlines of sexual practices and beliefs in the adult US population," which stands "in stunning contrast to the images of sexual excess or exaggeration that pervade the myriad sex reports appearing over the past forty years, all based on volunteer samples of the sexually interested and active."[47]

Respecting the role of commitment in sexual happiness, the report shows: that married people are "more emotionally satisfied with sex than the cohabiting partly because they are more emotionally invested; and that the emotional satisfaction and physical pleasure of single men and women were highest for those expecting the relationship to last a lifetime.[48] Professor Waite added that men or women who had another partner during the course of the year – in addition to their marital, cohabiting or primary dating partner – were less emotionally satisfied, as were those whose partner had another partner.[49]

This landmark study was confirmed in 2004 in another reliable study from the National Bureau of Economic Research, reviewing the General Social Survey of the United States. It concluded that married people have the most sex, and that the happiness-maximizing number of sex partners in a prior year is one.[50]

A more recent report on American's sexual preferences further contradicted sexual expressionism's self-centeredness. It showed that, for sexual partners, a mindset of interdependency and mutual gift delivers superior "results" than a mindset of self-gratification, identity-realization or autonomy. In short, the research indicated that individuals feel more sexual desire for their partner over a longer run when they care a great deal about him or her, and seek to please the other, not themselves. They are "motivated to meet their partner's sexual needs, even when these needs conflict with their own preferences."[51]

---

[46] Shere Hite, *The Hite Report* (New York: Seven Stories Press, 1976).
[47] Linda J. Waite and Kara Joyner, "Emotional and Physical Satisfaction with Sex in Married, Cohabiting, and Dating Sexual Unions: Do Men and Women Differ?" in *Sex, Love, and Health in America: Private Choices and Public Policies*, ed. Edward O. Laumann and Robert T. Michael (Chicago: the University of Chicago Press, 2001): 239–274, 240.
[48] *Id.* at 256.
[49] *Id.* at 257,
[50] David G. Blanchflower and Andrew J. Oswald, "Money, Sex and Happiness: An Empirical Study," NBER Working Paper, No. 10499 (2004) www.nber.org/papers/w10499.
[51] Amy Muise et al., "Keeping the Spark Alive: Being Motivated to Meet a Partner's Sexual Needs Sustains Sexual Desire in Long-Term Romantic Relationships," *Social Psychological and Personality Science* 4 (2013) 267–273.

Getting Women Wrong

Frequently it is argued that sexual expressionism is necessary to destroy the double standard, and to free women from disproportionate care of children, and the role-limitations that accompany this. The federal government offers to accomplish these ends by assimilating women to the male norm: sex without childbirth, by means of either contraception or abortion. Yet one of the clearest themes emerging from modern scholarly and popular literature is the failure of sexual expression to reflect and advance women. Logically, and even historically, this is not surprising. Why would sex be the only domain in which justice for women is perfectly achieved by conforming women to men's preferences and outcomes?

There is a strong case that the federal government's failure to "read" women correctly begins with its failure to acknowledge relevant differences between men and women in the sexual realm. Although a case for inquiring about sex differences regarding sex almost certainly has to begin by acknowledging the widespread suspicion that such an inquiry is tantamount to an invitation to subordinate women.

Feminist icon Gloria Steinem famously replied to the news that the National Institutes of Health intended to research sex differences between men and women by saying: "[i]t's anti-American, crazy thinking to do this kind of research"[52] University of California neuroscientist Larry Cahill reported that he was warned by his peers not to study sex differences because it would "kill" his career. He reports, however, that even medical researchers who are reluctant to accept *other* differences between men and women, easily accept evidence about their differences respecting sexual expression.[53]

An inquiry into sex differences does not inevitably precipitate ranking. In fact, in the face of emerging scientific data about sex differences, and evidence that women are harmed by one-size-fits-all policies, it seems more likely that identifying differences would lead to greater fairness, not repression. Psychologist Carol Gilligan, for example, famously illustrated how the science of moral development was both impoverished and unfair to women by its failure to incorporate women's persistent inclination to take third-party needs into account when reaching moral judgments.[54]

[52] John Stossel, "War on Women," *Townhall*, March 12, 2014, www.townhall.com/columnists/johnstossel/2014/03/12/war-on-women-n1807016.
[53] Larry Cahill, "Equal≠The Same: Sex Differences in the Human Brain," *Cerebrum* (March-April 2014) www.ncbi.nlm.nih.gov/pmc/articles/PMC4087190.
[54] Carol Gilligan, *In a Different Voice: Psychological Theory and Women's Development* (Cambridge: Harvard University Press, 1982).

Medicine, too, is an area in which acknowledging sex differences has led to progress for women. It has become increasingly acceptable for neurologists and geneticists to speak about sex differences, in pursuit of better treatment for women.

Observed differences between men and women are not just hormonal, but also genetic, and the result of gene/environment interactions. Some behavioral differences are even manifest within hours or days after birth. In fact the most consistent findings regularly concern differences respecting aggression, nurturance of others and sexuality.[55] In 1990, the National Institutes of Health established its Office of Research on Women's Health. And in 1993 Congress required NIH-funded clinical research to include female subjects so that its findings might be safely applied to women. Neuroscientist Dr. Cahill summarizes how sexual equality is better promoted by this new norm:

> Women and men are *not* being treated equally, because by and large, women are being treated as if they were the same as men. To make real progress in improving *both* men's and women's health, ... we need neuroscientist and non-neuroscientist alike to determine whether they too operate on the false assumption that "equal" means "the same." If so, toss that assumption aside. True equality for the sexes demands it.[56]

Men's and women's sexual choices manifest their differences. For example, a large number of studies show that women have fewer lifetime sexual partners than men and report a desire for fewer partners. Women are less interested in casual sex, as has been illustrated more than a few times by experiments demonstrating men's greater willingness to agree to sex with a stranger. A 2015 paper in the *Archives of Sexual Behavior*,[57] reported that, while rates of casual (sometimes called "non-partner") sex have increased, men report more encounters than women, and depending upon age cohorts, sometimes by rates approaching two to one.

Studies of sex ratios and sexual behavior in 117 countries also show that, where women control a mating "market" – that is, where women are more scarce – couples are more monogamous and oriented toward long-term mating. The opposite happens in settings where men are scarcer.[58]

---

[55] Melvin Konner, *The Evolution of Childhood: Relationships, Emotion, Mind* (Cambridge, Massachusetts: The Belknap Press of Harvard University), 261–62, 63.

[56] Cahill, "Equal≠The Same: Sex Differences in the Human Brain."

[57] Jean M. Twenge et al., "Changes in American Adults' Sexual Behavior and Attitudes, 1972–2012," *Archives of Sexual Behavior* 44 (2015): 2273–2285.

[58] John Angrist, "How Do Sex Ratios Affect Marriage and Labor Markets? Evidence from America's Second Generation," *Quarterly Journal of Economics* 117 (2002): 997–1038.

Men also display lower levels of emotional investment and sexual exclusivity than women. Men are less likely than women to strongly believe that they would not have sex unless they were in love, and that affairs are always wrong. Men are more likely than women to find the idea of sex with a stranger or a group sex appealing.[59] Finally, men are more likely to masturbate or to conduct multiple sexual relationships simultaneously.

Women, on the other hand, require a "longer minimum commitment than do men in order to consider a relationship permanent enough. Women tend to be satisfied with nothing less than a lifetime commitment, whereas men make less of a distinction between a relationship that they expect to last several years and one that they expect to last a lifetime."[60]

Women's on-average greater desire for commitment, and their higher levels of guilt respecting nonmarital sex, were confirmed in a 1993 meta-analysis of 177 studies, conducted from the 1960s to the 1980s, and involving a total of 58,000 men and over 69,000 women.[61] Substantial differences in attitudes on these matters remained fairly constant over time. The authors were surprised, given what they described as women's ability to "engage in sex with little fear of pregnancy." They concluded, however that there are likely intrinsic differences affecting women's attitudes and practices. Another meta-analysis, published in 2003, with 118 collaborating authors studying 52 nations, concluded that, while women will sometimes engage in short-term mating strategies, men are much more interested in a greater number and variety of partners, no matter whether they are single or married, gay or straight.[62]

Other empirically observed differences between men and women concern their sexual fantasies: women fantasize more about romantic relationships and commitment, and men more about bodily sex.[63] Men and women have also demonstrated dramatically different levels of interest in medicine treating "sexual dysfunction." In the first month that Viagra was on the market,

---

[59] See, e.g., Russell D. Clark and Elaine Hatfield, "Gender Differences in Receptivity to Sexual Offers," *Journal of Psychology and Human Sexuality* 2 (1989): 39–55; and see Lisa Taddeo, "I Went Undercover on America's Cheating Website," *Redbook*, March 30, 2011 www.redbookmag.com/love-sex/relationships/advice/a11620/cheating-websites.

[60] Waite and Joyner, "Emotional and Physical Satisfaction with Sex in Married, Cohabiting, and Dating Sexual Unions: Do Men and Women Differ," 265.

[61] Mary Beth Oliver and Janet Shibley Hyde, "Gender Differences in Sexuality: A Meta-Analysis," *Psychological Bulletin* 114 (1993): 29–51.

[62] David Schmitt et al., "Universal Sex Differences in the Desire for Sexual Variety: Tests from 52 Nations, 6 Continents and 13 Islands," *Journal of Personality and Social Psychology* 85 (2003): 85–103, www.bradley.edu/dotAsset/163311.pdf.

[63] Sarah Murnen, Carrie Wright, and Gretche Kaluzny, "A Meta-Analytic Review of the Research that Relates Masculine Ideology to Sexual Aggression," *Sex Roles* 46 (2002): 359–375.

doctors wrote about 1.5 million prescriptions, as compared with under 300 prescriptions for women's "pink pill."[64]

Qualitative reports from books about the "hookup" culture among young adults, confirm the quantitative material above. The books follow a familiar pattern. Outrageous stories of humiliating or depersonalized nonrelationship sex are reported, alongside claims by some young women or men that even these events are fun, empowering, instructive, or better than getting romantically serious too young.[65] At the same time, all of the authors eventually conclude that women are regularly less satisfied than men with casual sex. They show that women will consider having sex to attempt to "jump-start" a relationship, while men retain the power to decide if a hookup will become something more. Women express the feeling that the relationship market is outside their control, thus not really governed by the principle of consent.[66] Not infrequently, they report that the sex is not fully voluntary, or at least not fully desired. Sociologist Kathleen Bogle's account reported that only one-third of young women said they truly wanted to have sex the first time, versus 50 percent of young men.[67] Authors Peggy Orenstein and Donna Freitas report that women more often wish they had waited longer, and feel unsatisfied with casual sex.[68]

These books also regularly include more accounts of sex that women sometimes regard as degrading or painful. This refers to anal sex, and oral sex –which one interviewee referred to as "homework"[69] – on men's request. Women also report more alcohol-fueled sex, and some depression because of the failed expectation that, if the sex was great, a great relationship would follow.[70]

It seems apparent based upon all of the above that in light of women's and men's divergent preferences and constraints, sexual expressionism risks harming women disproportionately. Women have fertility constraints that men do not share. Men are still expected to "do the asking" when it comes to dating

---

[64] Lizzie Crocker, "Why is No One Buying Female Viagra?" *The Daily Beast*, November 19, 2015, www.thedailybeast.com/articles/2015/11/19/why-is-no-one-buying-female-viagra.html.

[65] See, e.g. Peggy Orenstein, Girls and Sex; Laura Sessions Stepp, *Unhooked: How Young Women Pursue Sex, Delay Love and Lose at Both* (New York: Riverhead Books, 2007); and Kathleen A. Bogle, *Hooking Up: Sex, Dating and Relationships on Campus* (New York: New York University Press, 2008).

[66] Bogle, *Hooking Up*, 173, 180. 185.

[67] Id., 8–9.

[68] Orenstein, *Girls and Sex*, 107, 221; Donna Freitas, *The End of Sex* (New York: Basic Books, 2013), 104–105.

[69] Orenstein, *Girls and Sex*, 55; Freitas, *The End of Sex*, 40–46, 50–51, 82–85.

[70] Sessions Stepp, *Unhooked: How Young Women Pursue Sex, Delay Love and Lose at Both*, 155.

and marriage. Sex is divorced from even the ideas of children or an ongoing relationship. Nonmarital sex outside of a relationship is more common. Women, more often than men, feel pressured to engage in it in order to stir the possibility of a relationship. Men do not feel pressured to marry, even in the event of a pregnancy, given the availability of abortion and the large decline in the stigma attached to unwed mothering.

Economist Tim Reichert depicts the dynamics summarized above as a "prisoner's dilemma" for women.[71] He begins his analysis by showing that in the United States today, there are fewer people participating in the marriage market by age thirty. They are, however, participating in the sex market. Because of women's fertility constraints, and perhaps also because of evolutionary inclinations, however, the following situation arises: the average age at which men exit the sex market and enter the marriage market is higher than the average age at which women make the same decision. This, in turn, means that at each point in time, more men will inhabit the sex market than women. Women will therefore have less bargaining power in the marriage market than in the sex market. In the sex market, women will experience a "prisoner's dilemma" which he describes as "any social setting wherein all parties have a choice between cooperation and noncooperation, and where all parties would be better off if they chose cooperation. But because people in a prisoner's dilemma setting cannot effectively coordinate and enforce cooperation, all parties choose the best individual choice, which is noncooperation. The social result is disastrous and everyone is made poorer."

Reichert concludes that women in the sex market can command a "high price" and are inclined to join in one by one – perhaps to meet their future spouse – when in fact, they would be better off as a group were they to cooperate, in order to advantage themselves more in the marriage market.

Even the book that gives the most positive initial endorsement of sexual expressionism as freedom, pleasure and choice for women – Steven Seidman's *Romantic Longings* – concludes equivocally. After claiming that consent, together with attention to women's pleasure, equal sexual fairness, Seidman acknowledges that a great deal of evidence indicates that women want more romance and intimacy with their sex. He also worries about the potential for the new sexual freedoms to cause women to suffer abuse, pregnancy, nonmarital births and poverty, among other problems.[72]

---

[71] Tim Reichert, "Bitter Pill," *First Things*, May 2010, www.firstthings.com/article/2010/05/bitter-pill.

[72] Seidman, *Romantic Longings*, 104–108, 130, 136, 143, 148, 153, 155.

Perhaps the best distillations of women's situation in a context of sexual expressionism are offered by sociologist Eva Illouz, in her writing about the "transformation of the ecology and architecture of sexual choice" for women. She concludes that men have far more sexual and emotional choices in the modern market for relationships, and that while "middle class heterosexual women" have "never been so sovereign" respecting their bodies, they are "emotionally dominated by men in new and unprecedented ways."[73] She continues:

> If – as many agree – the cult of freedom in the economic realm can and does sometimes have devastating consequences – producing uncertainty and large income inequalities, for example – then we should at the very least similarly inquire about its consequences in the personal, emotional and sexual realms.... A radical mind should not shy away from examining and questioning the unintended consequences of one's deepest and most cherished norms and beliefs, here freedom.... In the same way that freedom in the economic realm creates inequalities, and makes them invisible, freedom in the sexual realm has had the same effect of obscuring the social conditions which make possible the emotional domination of men over women.[74]

Sexual expressionism works best for those who are more likely to endorse sex without marriage or another sign of serious commitment, are not biologically constrained regarding childbearing, who cannot be harmed by birth control drugs and devices, and who do not become pregnant or undergo abortions. It doesn't work well for women.

A CRITIQUE OF THE GOVERNMENT'S PROPOSED SOLUTIONS

Federal responses to nonmarital birth are also inadequate or ethically problematic when considered in light of the government's obligations to children and to adults.

I will begin with a consideration of the back door response and then move to the contraception programs. Here, an introductory caveat is necessary. As stated in Chapter Three, my critiques of existing back door efforts are not a rejection of their necessity. They are important as a matter of satisfying ethical duties to children and promoting the common good. While they are necessary, however, they are not sufficient, and surely do not obviate the responsibility

---

[73] Eva Illouz, *Why Love Hurts* (Cambridge: Polity Press, 2012), 241, 239.
[74] *Id.*, 240.

of adults privately, or the state publicly, to act to protect children at the time of conception.

My critique of the record of governmental social programs is also not a criticism of nonmarital children or families. It is possible – and indeed more consistent – to affirm the need to assist children who are disadvantaged in part due to their family structure, while working to avoid this situation for later-born children. I recommend that the government adopt this stance as well, in place of it current messaging about sex and marriage and children. This approach fits comfortably within both of the classic strands of children's advocacy: parents' and the state's responsibilities to protect vulnerable children; and empowering children to realize their capacities and freedom over the long run.

BACK DOOR CRITIQUE

Other People's Children

The government's decision to lean so heavily on back door solutions, and not front-door interventions directly addressed to nonmarital births, reflects at best a naïve and at worst an indifferent view of human inclinations. It is remarkably easier to ask parents to care for their own children than to inspire people to care for others' children. No matter the source of this widely observed fact, it should inform government policy on family structure.

Back door programs encourage altruism toward vulnerable – including nonmarital – children. Yet, by taking a sexual expressionist view, the government is simultaneously communicating that when parents are conceiving their own children, above all, they should consult only or primarily their own inclinations and judgments about sex and about children's family structure. This is a recipe for undercutting citizen support for the edifice of social welfare programs serving children. It would be better for the state to broadcast *both* that it is working to link sex with parental responsibility for the good of children, *and* that all children deserve social solicitude.

Too Little too Late

Knowledge about what succeeds and what fails to assist nonmarital children creates a duty. The literature is clear that marriage works better for children. It helps even before their birth, and during the crucial early years when the child's brain is developing. It lays the groundwork for the child's later capacities and achievements. This is accepted wisdom in the education, neurologic, sociological and economic fields, as described in Chapters Two and Three.

This ethical principle is endorsed by the Institute of Medicine in its report to Congress about early childhood development entitled *From Neurons to Neighborhoods*. After showcasing the evidence about the effects of children's prenatal and infant environments upon life-long chances, it referred to a "convergence of advancing knowledge and changing circumstances call[ing] for a fundamental reexamination of the nation's responses to the needs of young children and their families, many of which were formulated several decades ago." The "nation has not … capitalized sufficiently on the knowledge that has been gained from nearly half a century of considerable public investment in research."[75]

The federal government is specifically aware of children's need for consistent, positive, and plentiful interactions with parents in the earliest years. It has responded to the evidence with programs attempting to meet children's needs at earlier and earlier periods of their lives. It began Head Start in 1965, and later Early Head Start, which was followed by home visiting programs such as Nurse Family Partnerships in 2009. Home visiting programs assist mothers and children even before birth. A current federal experiment involves expanding the focus of the nurse–mother visiting program to secure more cooperative father involvement throughout.[76] The federal government needs to continue along this path. Reversing sexual expressionism is the beginning. Attending to child welfare at conception should be next.

CONTRACEPTION CRITIQUE

As discussed in the Introduction, it is not surprising that so many believe that federal contraception programs answer a central problem raised by this book: the government's inadequate attention or even reckless indifference to the link between children's welfare and marital parenthood.

Anticipating that this would be a common response, I addressed this topic at length in Chapter One by pointing to the following: the federal focus on unintended pregnancies and not children's welfare; the coincidence of federal

75 National Research Council and Institute of Medicine, *From Neurons to Neighborhoods: the Science of Early Childhood Development* (Committee on Integrating the Science of Early Childhood Development, Board on Children, Youth, and Families), ed. Jack P. Shonkoff and Deborah A. Phillips (Washington DC, National Academy Press, 2000), 2.

76 Heather Sandstrom et al., *Serving Young Fathers in Home Visiting Programs: Highlights from a Research Study* (OPRE Report 2015–105) (November 2015), www.acf.hhs.gov/sites/default/files/opre/20151124_serving_young_fathers_in_home_visiting_programs_brief.pdf.

programs with dramatic rises in nonmarital births; federal silence in the face of possible risk compensation effects; and the undermining of parents' responsibility for children and the parents' own stable relations, communicated by the mantra "unprotected sex makes babies."

Here I will consider those aspects of federal contraception programs raising ethical problems, to further confirm that contraception programs are insufficiently responsible to children or even undermining of children's interests. Each critique should be considered against the backdrop of my proposed standard that law and policy should work to urge the adults who create children to take responsibility at the moment family structure begins.

Forgetting Children

Many believe that the government's "safe/protected sex" messaging pays sufficient attention to children at the front door of family formation. It hopes to persuade parents to have a child only when they "intend" to, which often but not consistently means during marriage. I have discussed already why this is insufficient *de facto*, even while it is true by definition that birth control can and regularly does prevent conception or birth when a woman or man employs it correctly. This is, however, a narrow, and overly technical perspective on birth control, insensitive to the context in which it is actually used and ultimately forgetful or even dismissive of children's claims. Federal birth control policy therefore cannot render sexual expressionism sufficiently child-protective.

Separating children out of sex – as discussed above in my critique of sexual expressionism – leads naturally to isolating adults' interests in sex. Anthony Giddens was right. Wanting a child, or thinking about whether or not the parents will together raise the child, becomes a wholly separate matter from the sex itself.[77] Thus it is not surprising that, by the time the Supreme Court arrived at questions relating to sex-followed-by-abortion or same-sex marriage with no possibility for procreation, it spoke repeatedly of sex as a matter of individual identity formation and emotional happiness.

I have already discussed above and at length the ways in which the notional separation of sex and children can undercut parents' stability and obscure their communications with one another. I will add a few additional comments here about how birth control might distance parents from the norm of responsibility to their children.

---

[77] Giddens, *The Transformation of Intimacy*, 174.

Birth control distances sexual partners from the children they have "by accident" while using birth control, and even children they have "on purpose." Contraception programs, with their ubiquitous messages that "unprotected sex" makes babies and disease, imply that children are "made" by some force called "unprotected sex." "Unprotected sex" might mean method failure, in which case the pharmaceutical company that made the deficient or difficult-to-use product, "made" the baby. Method failure might also pin responsibility upon the doctor who failed to properly insert or educate about the contraception. A birth to a woman who possessed contraception also indicts the woman who refused, forgot or misused it. In every case the subtext and the text of "unprotected sex" is "blame." Babies are the result of someone's failure.

This is completely contrary to the notion, without contraception so dominating the picture, that "sex makes babies." When sex makes babies, not "unprotected sex," responsibility is easily assigned. The sexual partners did it.

Over time, as discussed above, it seems more likely that when adults live as if children are wholly separate from sex, they become less disposed toward or prepared for them, or familiar with the idea that they should understand sexual relationships as a bond with another person who will be mother or father to one's common child. Several of the "hookup" genre books note that young women, formed in college by practicing contracepted sex with uncommitted partners, later experience difficulties moving into new ways of "doing sex" and relationships after college. Laura Sessions Stepp and Donna Freitas, for example, write about college experiences potentially compromising women's ability to sustain commitment,[78] or their teaching women to deaden feelings for sexual partners as a necessary defense against future disappointment.[79]

I should conclude this section on how contraception "disappears" children from the horizon, by noting that my objection is not equivalent to claiming that sex is strictly about or for procreation. This is a common reaction against any criticism of contraception. Of course, sex is always about the relationship between the couple. To say otherwise is to demean human will and human choices involving highly personal and significant interactions and communications. I discuss this at some length in the Introduction, and in Chapter One. At the very same time, however, given the striking fact that sex is also the behavior by which human beings are created – and by which their family lives are importantly shaped – it is necessary to remind sexual partners that sex is naturally procreative.

[78] Sessions Stepp, *Unhooked*, 7.
[79] Freitas, *The End of Sex*, 67–68; Sessions Stepp, *Unhooked*, 82.

Technology Compromising Women's Health,
and Problematizing Pregnancy

Even at the dawn of the modern birth control movement, social observers worried about the power that it could exert precisely as technology. Social critic Walter Lippmann, for example, observed in 1929 that the birth control reformers would remake all human relations – dating, marriage, sex – in accordance with the logic of birth control, and leave to the side the matter of human nature.[80] Ahead of his time, he understood that birth control provokes the "technological imperative" – the notion that new human inventions are both inevitable and positive for humanity.

On the theme of birth control as technology, there are several important aspects to explore. First, in light of birth control's potential impacts on women's health, as described in Chapter Three, women are owed full information about the side and health effects of different forms of contraception. It appears that the federal government is not as forthcoming as necessary, especially regarding the link between hormonal contraception and depression, and the links between Depo Provera and HIV transmission and bone density loss. This suggests a stronger interest in avoiding pregnancies following sexual expression than in women's health.

A separate matter for an "informed consent" critique, is the government's failure to articulate carefully the difference between drugs and devices which can prevent fertilization, and those which act to destroy an already formed and developing human embryo (usually by thinning the lining of the uterus so that the embryo cannot embed). This is a profoundly important distinction. In the words of feminist author Germaine Greer: "Whether you feel that the creation and wastage of so many embryos is an important issue or not, you must see that the cynical deception of millions of women by selling abortifacients as if they were contraceptives is incompatible with the respect due to women as human beings."[81]

Another ethical matter concerning women's well-being involves the credible argument that contraception has affected the markets for both sex and marriage, to the detriment of women. The argument has the virtue of appealing to common sense, and accounting for women's personal testimony. It also has support from respected economists and sociologists. If an actor – here the government – is promoting a position affecting an environment, then he or

---

[80]   Walter Lippmann, *A Preface to Morals* (St. Louis: Transaction Publishers, 1982), 293–301.
[81]   Germaine Greer, *The Whole Woman* (New York: Alfred A. Knopf, 2005), 99.

she ought to take proportionate responsibility for the consequences. This is an increasingly well-accepted norm applicable to the natural environment. It ought to be extended to those human environments that influence the choices and outcomes of sex, marriage and parenting. To use the framework of Hans Jonas, we should be asking what new responsibilities are "commensurate" with the technological power of contraception and the government's valorization of contraception as justice toward children and freedom for women.[82]

In the context of the natural environment, the federal government regularly understands the imperative to act where individual citizens or institutions lack the incentives to alter their behavior to sufficiently curb pollution or climate change. Likewise, regarding the effects upon women of the market for sex and marriage structured in part by contraception – and strengthened by governmental endorsement – the government has a responsibility. It should cease exacerbating women's situation, and also work to improve the environment. I offer suggestions in this vein in Chapter Five.

Another ethical inquiry applicable to contraception as technology concerns the "meanings" or "messages" conveyed by the manner in which contraception acts on human beings. Meanings are also conveyed by the messages attached to a technology by its promoters.

As already noted above, and elaborated in the work of Anthony Giddens, by its very actions and effects, contraception communicates that sex is about the adult partners and not about making babies. The technological imperative associated with contraception also means that sex without pregnancy is not only superior to older, natural methods of avoiding pregnancy, but also superior to sex *with* pregnancy. In other words, it conveys that nonprocreative sex is a more advanced or desirable kind of sex. The paradigm of "medicine and health" that the government applies to contraception further suggests also that a contracepted woman is "healthier."

Contraception understood as technological progress also casts a shadow upon children – at least until an adult has certified a child's "intendedness." As Zygmunt Bauman and others have observed, it shifts the notion of a child away from the categories of "gift" "wonder" and "gratitude" and toward "choice."[83] Furthermore, everything that is associated with pregnancy – eggs, women, women's fertility, and parenting – is also problematized.[84]

---

[82] Jonas, *The Imperative of Responsibility*, ix, x.

[83] See Bauman, *Liquid Love*, 46, 47; see also Helen M. Alvaré, "Same-Sex Marriage and the 'Reconceiving' of Children," *Case Western Reserve Law Review* 64 (2014): 830–862, (discussing the work of Marcel Gauchet in Marcel Gauchet, "L'Enfant du Désir," *Champ Psychomatique* 47 (2007): 9).

[84] Brian Brock, *Christian Ethics in a Technological Age* (Grand Rapids: Eerdmans, 2010), 152.

Contraception's constant association with the health and freedom norm of "intended pregnancy," also implies that children who are chosen are superior to children who are not. It spotlights adults' evaluation of children's value. This is ironic, given that sexual expressionism was intended to be the polar opposite of a legal regime in which "illegitimacy" law separated respectable from unrespectable mothers and children. The new legal regime – with its language of intended and unintended children – simply substitutes a mother's evaluation of the child's worth for the state's evaluation. Either way, the child is evaluated, and regularly found wanting.

Other language used to describe or promote contraception is also subject to ethical evaluation, as is the very form of contraception.[85] According to the federal government, contraception is "healthcare." It is "prescribed" by doctors or bought at pharmacies. It comes in the form of pills or shots or devices, many of which must be inserted and removed in medical settings. This too implies that being sterile is a health enhancement, and that being fertile is less healthy, or even unhealthy.

The language of contraception as "protection" or "safe sex" has further implications, both for male/female relations and for children. It suggests that women need protection from men and from children. More harshly, it evokes the idea that children can be an assault on a defensive barricade. This mental picture is even more vivid in connection with current recommendations to women using LARCs that they should arm themselves with two forms of "protection," because LARCs are ineffective against sexually transmitted infections. One imagines a soldier preparing to do battle, not a lover or a spouse or a parent.

The needs that contraceptive technology claims to answer are also a matter for ethical evaluation.[86] Contraception was first offered on a larger scale by the federal government, in connection with combatting a claimed "population bomb," along with rising nonmarital birthrates among the poor. Then, although more so today, contraception became closely associated with women's freedom and equality – freedom from fertility, which means freedom from children. In one of the first marketing efforts for the pill, its pharmaceutical manufacturer, G. D. Searle, delivered to doctors a paperweight of a naked, gold-painted, bare-breasted woman – Andromeda – with her head up, breaking free from her chains. On her back appeared the word "unfettered."[87]

---

[85] Brian Brock, *Christian Ethics in a Technological Age* (Grand Rapids: Eerdmans, 2010).

[86] *Id.*, 163.

[87] Jonathan Eig, *The Birth of the Pill: How Four Crusaders Reinvented Sex and Launched A Revolution* (New York: W.W. Norton and Co., 2014), 302–303.

At the same time contraception was entering the scene on these terms, children had become consumers, not producers, in the family economy. Together, these realities negatively influenced the valuation of children. Bauman has noted how, following the possibility that the cost of children could be *avoided* by means of contraception, *welcoming* children became a kind of "consumption." The consumers, their parents, are invited to consider whether the emotional consumption they are getting is justified by the huge risks they are taking.[88] Bauman adds that children are further "consumerized" today because they are equally obtainable from science and from sex. In fact this raises the further question of seeking to consume only attractive children.[89]

As described above, the federal government, leading scholars and medical associations and interest groups are currently, stridently promoting LARCs. LARC usage is rising, although there will always be a number of women who dislike their invasiveness, or fear their side effects. There will always be women who are at special risk because of their age, or weight, or their smoking, or suffering health conditions contraindicating for LARCs. There will be women of color who are sensitive to any indication that the government is "targeting" them with longer acting birth control.

Setting aside these groups, however, we should ask whether there are ethical difficulties for the remaining groups of women, additional to those difficulties applicable to birth control technology generally? I think the answer is yes, even as there are great expectations associated with their more widespread use: allowing uncommitted sexual expression, while also protecting children, women, and the poor, all in one fell swoop.

LARCs, as a technology, pose additional elements for ethical consideration, given their greater potential to temporarily sterilize vast numbers of single women. Like contraception generally, LARCs also act to fracture links between men and women, and between parents and children. LARCs, however, double down on this separation, due to widespread belief in, and promotion of, their effectiveness.

LARCs also do nothing to encourage men to value women, or committed relationships or children. They raise the possibility that women's "default" position – as infertile – will reduce the hurdle of their making separate, independent decisions about becoming sexually involved with particular partners over the course of the many years during which LARCs are effective. Reversing women's "default" from fertility to nonfertility is precisely why scholar Isabella Sawhill

---

[88] Bauman, *Liquid Love*, 42–43.
[89] Id., 40.

so strongly recommends LARCs.[90] This is not to say that critics of LARCs are claiming that women using them will have sex with anyone who asks. This is not a serious argument. It is only to say that the already increasing practice of nonrelationship or casual sex – which ordinarily requires women using ordinary birth control to decide about sexual involvement a day or a week at a time – could be further facilitated by LARCs. Having additional sexual partners before marriage does not usually bode well for marriage quality or stability. In the words of Sarah McLanahan, while she endorses LARCs as a means of reducing poverty, and hopes they would help parents more ready to take on parenting, she is "not certain it would restore marriage as the standard way of raising children"[91] This is a significant understatement.

LARCs rather have the potential to more forcefully divorce sex from ideas about the good of partners' stable unions and their jointly welcoming and caring for children. What is rather needed are efforts to capacitate couples to take joint responsibility for their children, not to assist them to forget them further. LARCs promotion as currently imagined could easily encourage the latter.

There is also the possibility that LARCs will harden opposition to children by means of the expectation of their very low failure rates. The abortion ratios in the St. Louis LARCs project seem to bear this out. When a large percentage of women were persuaded to trade "less effective" forms of birth control for LARCs, abortion ratios (abortions per pregnancy) were nearly 100 percent, four times the national average. How does this capacitate a couple to accept joint responsibility for a child?

Finally, LARCs' effectiveness – alongside their requiring medical application and removal – make them a particularly powerful technology in the hands of government.[92] Even LARCs supporters have observed this for many years.[93] This could be an ethical concern, in connection with promotion of LARCs to the poor. Already Depo Provera, for example – with its potential for depression, bone density loss, and increased HIV transmission – is administered much more often to less-advantaged women and girls. Among African-American single women, over 33 percent have used it; among White

---

[90] Isabel Sawhill, *Generation Unbound: Drifting into Sex and Parenthood without Marriage* (Washington, DC: Brookings Institution Press, 2014).

[91] Sara McLanahan and Isabel Sawhill, "Marriage and Child Well Being Revisited: Introducing the Issue," *The Future of Children* 25 (Fall 2015): 9.

[92] Ellen H. Moskowik et al., "Long-Acting Contraceptives: Ethical Guidance for Policymakers and Health Care Providers," *The Hastings Center Report* (January 2, 1995), www.onlinelibrary.wiley.com/doi/10.2307/3562503/pdf.

[93] Jenny A. Higgins, "Celebration Meets Cautions, LARC's Boons, Potential Busts and the Benefits of a Reproductive Justice Approach," *Contraception* 89 (2014): 237–241.

women, only 20 percent.[94] Among women with a college education or more, about 12 percent have ever used Depo Provera; among women without a high school diploma or GED, 36 percent.[95] Minority women already report feeling pushed by doctors to use "more effective" birth control;[96] in fact, they do use it more than white women.

In sum, given more than 50 years of experience with widespread contraception, and reflecting on its messages and outcomes, a contraception strategy, including a LARCs strategy, is not a sufficiently child-oriented solution. In fact, as currently envisioned, it might easily further undermine children's welfare by undermining the stability of male/female relationships and their capacity for joint and generous parenting.

Having considered the anthropological mistakes and the ethical shortcomings of the federal government's current responses to nonmarital births, the next chapter offers several proposals to reverse sexual expressionism, and to put children's interests before adults', beginning at children's conception.

[94] US Centers for Disease Control, *Contraceptive methods women have ever used: United States, 1982–2010,* by Kimberly Daniels et al., U. S. Centers for Disease Control (2013), Table 2. Number of sexually experienced women aged 15–44 and percentage who have ever used the selected contraceptive method, by Hispanic origin and nativity and race: United States, 2006–2010.

[95] *Id.,* Table 3. Number of sexually experienced women aged 22–44, and percentage who have ever used the selected contraceptive method, by education: United States, 2006–2010, www.cdc.gov/nchs/data/nhsr/nhsr062.pdf.

[96] Higgins, "Celebration Meets Caution."

5

Conclusion and Recommendations

This book builds on existing scholarship about the emphasis on individual sexual expression in the current legal and cultural environment. It also builds on scholarship about the difficulties faced by children born apart from marriage. It links these two, while also differing from a great deal of existing literature in its emphasis on the problems of separating sexual expression from the idea of caring for children. This separation also isolates the partners' sexual relationship from thoughts about their relationship as whole persons, and from thoughts of tomorrow – of married life, of co-parenting. This, too, redounds to children's disadvantage by discouraging the partners' stable relations.

My thinking is informed by several outstanding features of the current moment in time. The federal government's affirmation of adult sexual expression performs some useful work – for sexual health and for women's equality in particular. We are well rid of the earlier legal regime punishing children for the circumstances of their birth. Federal willingness to offer substantial assistance to vulnerable fellow citizens, without discrimination according to family form, is just and necessary.

At the same time, however, the government has wildly overshot its goals of overturning unhealthy views on sex, and ending discrimination against women and nonmarital children. It is vaunting adult sexual expression in emotional terms with inadequate attention, even reckless indifference, to the wellbeing of children. It is ramping up demands and expectations regarding sexual expression by tying it to profound individual goods, such as identity-realization, personhood, dignity and happiness. This was comically observed the day after the *Obergefell* decision in a *New York Times* column, wherein the single writer asked if his life was now officially, legally meaningless because there was (to borrow a phrase from the decision) no one to answer his "lonely ... call" at night.[1]

The federal government persists in promoting "sexual expressionism" at a time when it is well agreed that marital parenting advantages children on average, and that gaps in marital parenting are provoking morally troubling gaps between races, classes and the sexes.

Sexual expressionism ignores the reality that children's family structure is routinely established at conception. It also ignores the possibility that sexual expressionism promotes the psychological, emotional, and intellectual separation of parents from children, and women from men, and thereby actually decapacitates adults for the enterprise of stable marriage and joint, marital parenting.

One can also observe at this time that federal social welfare programs are addressing increasingly granular needs of children and families who lack a second, stably invested biological parent in the home. These programs benefit from great good will, commendable expertise, and large budgets, albeit not as large as many would like. Yet they have proved inadequate to the task of helping children and families break the cycles of poverty, low education and nonmarital childbearing. They seem unable to build healthy, economically self-sufficient and employment-ready families for our twenty-first century world.

As we approach 60 years after the pill, and 50 years from the first major federal birth control program, one can further see that contraception has not achieved even the government's limited goal of reducing "unintended pregnancies." Nonmarital births have also increased substantially during this time, and the highest rates of both unintended and nonmarital births are among the groups receiving the most free, government-supported contraception. The list of government efforts in the contraception arena is long: it funds research about new or safer messages; it facilitates stocking the most effective contraceptives in convenient places; it gives contraception away to the poor, and commands private institutions to insure it without a co-pay for every other group; it withstands hundreds of lawsuits to require religious conscientious objectors to do likewise; it exhorts doctors to have contraception to hand the minute a woman's labor and delivery is over; and it paves the way for even very young women to obtain contraception at pharmacies and schools and clinics.

[1]   Michael Cobb, "The Supreme Court's Lonely Hearts Club," *The New York Times*, June 30, 2015, www.nytimes.com/2015/06/30/opinion/the-supreme-courts-lonely-hearts-club .html?_r=0.

Yet women continue to have misgivings about contraception's health and side effects. They have personal reasons for not wanting to use it with certain partners, or in light of the sex and marriage markets in their particular communities. They forget it or use it incorrectly. They want children.

Long-acting reversible contraceptives or LARCs can address a small portion of these objections, but they raise important health and ethical questions of their own. Scholars from a wide variety of disciplines concur that, whether we are talking about more or less effective contraception, it is likely that contraception, and also abortion, have created new markets for sex and marriage which are simply more likely to produce more nonmarital sex, less marriage and a higher number of nonmarital births.

The federal government's approach is neither practically nor ethically sufficient for children, nor for women and the poor. It has pursued its current approach for a long time. It is time to improve and readjust. Social welfare programs at the "back door" need to continue, and to continue improving. Programs for the youngest children likely require even more emphasis and funding than they presently receive. They may also benefit from efforts to include fathers early and often in the project of joint parenting.

Yet the government should also cease broadcasting sexual expressionism. And it should go much further, and alter existing programs which address citizens – adults and teens alike – at or about the time of a child's conception, so as to take account of the child's needs. The burden of proof today is on those who would oppose additional, even unconventional, efforts to assist children from the beginning, when the family structure begins.

Of course, there is no simple or even noncontroversial answer to the enormous challenge of unmarried adults' interest in sexual expression, or in bearing children apart from marriage. It is a difficult topic for any author, as well as any policy maker. No one wants to be a modern Don Quixote, tilting at this particular windmill. Yet we cannot overlook that we have left a stone unturned – that at the very least, it would be helpful for the government to cease its preoccupation with adult sexual expression, and relink sex with the value of care for children. It would help further if there could be an honest reevaluation of the wisdom and efficacy of its two leading responses to the fallout for children.

Even though the problem I am addressing is monumental, my proposals are incremental because the terrain is so complex. As a lawyer, I am also aware that politics and inertia are powerful constraints.

Still, I believe that my proposals are more true to the aspirations especially of women and the poor regarding relationships and parenting. They might help children directly, and indirectly by way of helping their parents to enjoy more stable and fair relationships. They exhibit more common sense than the notion that we might build family stability on a framework of urging men and women having sex to forget for a long time about the possibility of building a secure relationship with one another, and to forget about children and their need for parents. They are more sensible than the idea that bureaucrats and programs – no matter how altruistic – can substitute for a mother and father's mutual regard and common care for their own children. My ideas are also continuous with the federal insight – interwoven silently but certainly in both its contraception and social welfare programs – that so much is lost when the second married parent is not on the scene. They are continuous with state family laws and policies, and newer family law proposals which seek to promote parents' joint care for their children. They are also in harmony with a demonstrated federal willingness to pursue logical ideas and programs, even if at first they do not succeed wildly. My proposals are as follows.

CONTINUE SOCIAL WELFARE PROGRAMS AT THE BACK DOOR

First, as indicated many times throughout this text, the federal government ought to continue assisting vulnerable children and families with current social welfare programs addressing the variety of topics I discussed in Chapter Three. For the reasons of justice and the common good I articulated there and in Chapter Four.

I realize that there is a literature which argues that generous social welfare might discourage marriage or marital childbearing, or even work. I cannot assess this in the space of this book. It is also not central to my proposal that the federal government reverse its sexual expressionism stance. I can say, however, that social welfare programs' *de facto* acknowledgment – by means of what they provide – of the elements of a well-functioning family, do not contradict my proposals at all.

I would also add that, to the extent possible, social welfare programs should become a vehicle for assisting parents as a couple, married or unmarried, when this is possible. This may help men and women understand the good of their partnership for the child, as distinguished from what each provides separately. It may also curb additional nonmarital fertility and multi-partner fertility. Of course, this excludes situations involving violence or other threats to a mother or child, but leaves room for federal action elsewhere. For example, the federal government should pursue its current attempts to incorporate fathers, and concern for the parents' relationship, into home visiting programs. It is also a good idea to establish child support at levels that do not feel punitive or impossible for poor men, in order to encourage father cooperation and visiting, and even possibly to further reduce further nonmarital fertility.[2]

CAPACITATE FOR MARRIAGE

A second proposal involves capacitating women and men for the possibility of marriage and marital parenting by improving their economic and employment prospects. We know that this is not a "silver bullet," but that it is a logical and humane solution worth trying. Americans, including the poor, desire marriage and prefer marital childbearing. Research indicates that the prospect of a living wage and a stable job may help more people feel empowered to marry and have marital children.[3] *Pace* my economist colleagues – arguments about the cost of these should take second place to arguments about their relationship to family formation among the poor, and to children's welfare.

It is both encouraging and discouraging how often one reads about ideas to capacitate disadvantaged Americans for marriage. Encouraging because the question stirs interest and ongoing, intelligent debate. Discouraging because so many good ideas have yet to be taken up on a scale that might make a difference. Given current data on family structure effects and given related income, wealth, and race gaps, it is certainly time to take up the cause of the poor with urgency, and with ideas favored by both left and right. These might include, *inter alia*: tailoring education in light of our future labor market; President Obama's idea about expanding and improving community colleges; lowering college costs; Professor Robert Lerman's proposals regarding apprenticeships;[4] an EITC which is both more generous, and more cognizant of the needs of married couples with children to avoid being unduly penalized for their two-income home; an increased minimum wage; and expanding the child tax credit and extending it to payroll taxes.

A very recent proposal to initiate a "universal basic income" is also worth investigating in light of the size and scope of our current poverty and family and employment problems, and in light of genuine doubts about solving these in a reasonable time. One of its leading proponents, union organizer Andy

---

[2] Irwin Garfinkel et al., "The Role of Child Support Enforcement and Welfare in Non-Marital Childbearing," *Journal of Population Economics* 16 (2003): 55–70.
[3] Sara McLanahan, "Diverging Destinies: How Children are Faring Under the Second Demographic Transition," *Demography* 41, no. 4 (2004): 618, 622.
[4] Robert I. Lerman, "Can Expanding Apprenticeship Strengthen American Families?" Institute for Family Studies, November 19, 2013, www.family-studies.org/can-expanding-apprenticeship-strengthen-american-families/.

Stern, calls it "raising the floor" in a book by the same name, and supports it in part, in the name of children's welfare.[5]

A universal basic income is a system in which the government provides every adult and child with a fixed income which does not begin to be reduced based upon the recipient's earned income, until he or she earns a certain amount, at which point it is essentially captured by higher marginal tax rates. It is beginning to generate prolific discussion[6] concerning its economic feasibility, and its effects upon the rest of the economy, including upon marriage and family life, though supporters point out it that might even boost work because, unlike means tested benefits, it would not be forfeited by working. The cost would be very high. Small scale "experiments" with a similar program are underway in Finland. Of course, it is unknown whether increased income would measurably assist people to consider marriage. Considering the current needs of lower-income Americans for both income and marriage, however, it is an idea worth further investigation.

PUTTING THE CHILD AT THE FRONT DOOR, WHICH MEANS PUTTING CHILDREN BACK INTO SEX

General Recommendations

My final set of recommendations directly addresses marital childbearing itself. I would go further than current scholars who rightly recommend a national campaign in favor of marital childbearing. I would explicitly articulate children's needs for stable, marital parenting *wherever* the government speaks about sex.

This is justified by the fact that the stability or instability of children's family structure is regularly begun at sex, at conception. It is also justified because it has not been tried, and there is an ethical imperative to prioritize children's needs. It is also more possible today than during an earlier period when sexual expressionism was being elaborated – because at that time we could not evaluate its outcomes, or the outcomes of programs designed to ameliorate its consequences.

[5]   Andy Stern, *Raising the Floor: How a Universal Basic Income Can Renew Our Economy and Rebuild the American Dream* (New York: Public Affairs 2016); see also Lareau, *Unequal Childhoods*, 252.
[6]   Eduardo Porter, "A Universal Basic Income is a Poor Tool to Fight Poverty," *New York Times*, May 31, 2016, https://www.nytimes.com/2016/06/01/business/economy/universal-basic-income-poverty.html?_r=0.

Furthermore, indirectly capacitating marital parenting with economic incentives is not enough. The retreat from marriage and marital parenting is not strictly a function of money. It is also influenced by ideas about sex and marriage and parenting – ideas that sexual expressionism and some contraception messaging promote. And our culture has been formed for so long on the basis of a separation of children from sex that nothing less than a direct conversation about this will do.

One of the advantages of injecting the question of children's welfare wherever "sex is spoken," is that the message will go out to well-off and poor citizens alike. I am sensitive to the criticism that the government is always lecturing the poor about sex and family life.

I will first describe the general contours of a new message, and then consider how to interweave this message into specific governmental programs.

To begin, the government ought to cease broadcasting sexual expressionism. It should rather state plainly that, while sexual expression is a healthy part of adult life, sex inescapably has a dual importance. It both bonds a couple and conceives children. Furthermore, children's family structure – marital or nonmarital – is usually established at conception. Finally, the government should regularly state that marital childbearing is the most stable and beneficial context for children, and therefore an important responsibility of parents. Children need the sexual partners who made them to be stably united. It should be added that, while it is possible children might receive benefits from long-term stable relations of parents other than marriage, these have not, to date, proved a sufficient substitute for marriage. This is not to insult adults performing loving and important care of their children, but rather to share an empirical fact about sexual partners' responsibility for the children.

The government and its partners may wish to add to this message that "remembering children" will not derogate from healthy adult sexual expression or happiness. It may even enrich sex by associating it with commitment – which both men and women like better, on average. This would also help men and women attain more stable marriages with fewer prior sex partners, which would benefit both adults and children.

The "warmth" of the government's language regarding children, and their relationship with united parents, should match or exceed the warmth of the government's prose regarding other aspects of sex. It matters. Who can forget the power of the rhetoric accompanying the campaign for same-sex marriage: "equal," and "love wins?"

This is all to say that when the government speaks about sex, it should first do no harm. It should cease encouraging citizens, in the words of Charles

Taylor, to continue to "live[] beyond our moral means."[7] It should cease promoting the foolish belief, in other words, that we can valorize individualism in the sexual arena, between men and women, and parents and children – while soon after demanding that when children are born, we must turn on a dime and embrace an ethic of solidarity, generosity, and even altruism toward our own children, and toward others'.

I further recommend that the government assume a particular tone, and employ certain categories in order to promote this message. It should cease implying that there is little hope for restoring marital childbearing among the less advantaged. Rather, it should adopt a civil rights tone, about empowering the disempowered – not only children, but also women who have been immiserated in the current sex and marriage marketplaces.

The government's tone should also be intelligent, and its statements full of relevant information. The federal government has enormous power to gather and to analyze data. It has shown this with its commitment to trying new and logical programs to assist citizens, to test these programs, report its findings, and continue to fund only "evidence based" programs. I would add that the government should not only rely on, but also fund large-scale studies about sex, marriage and parenting, given its capacity. Individuals within particular relationships, or even particular communities, cannot even see, let alone change, the current markets for sex and marriage. When this situation obtains – when a *system* is imposing costs that no one wishes to bear, but which create widespread suffering – *this* is the time for the government to step in: to inform and to aid individuals and communities to alter the larger environment. This is the situation regarding our natural environment: climate change is neither comprehensible nor alterable by a few. Neither is the current sexual environment.

Additionally, the government ought also to cease unnecessary rhetoric setting men against women. Without ceasing to work on domestic violence, rape or wage inequality, among other issues, it should also make the effort to emphasize the good of each sex, the unique and overlapping gifts of each sex, and the good of male/female synergies both in public and in private institutions.

These recommendations ought to be applied to every branch of government. Regarding the judiciary, private groups should inject them into lawsuits directly, if they are parties, or indirectly by way of amicus briefs. They should frame their arguments specifically as advocacy for the poor, or for women, children or families. Congress could include such recommendations

---

[7] Charles Taylor, *Sources of the Self: The Making of the Modern Identity*, 517.

in communications to the judiciary, in statutory declarations of purpose, and in briefs and arguments before federal courts, including the Supreme Court.

Specific Recommendations

Regarding specific executive and legislative policies and programs, I would propose the following – understanding, as with all federal proposals, that they should be subject to experiment, evaluation and reform.

I consider, first, sex education, because it is a place where the government speaks extensively about sex, via federally funded curricula. A look at the programs the government currently funds – some involving birth control education and others called "abstinence programs – reveals almost no significant attention to the life-long consequences for children of parents' creation of their family structure. Contraception-focused programs valorize consent, reducing risk, looking out for one's own future, consulting or clarifying personal values about "readiness" for sex, learning about one's own body, communicating with partners, and preventing pregnancy and disease.[8]

Even federally funded abstinence programs, do not appear to speak a great deal about children. Amidst a great deal of information about the benefits of abstinence for young men and women, federal law says only that abstinence programs can also teach that "bearing children out-of-wedlock is likely to have harmful consequences for the child, the child's parents, and society."[9]

My recommendation is to cease any sexual expressionist approach in all sex-education programs, and considerably ramp up information about the twofold reality of sex, including the fact that it regularly creates children's family structure, which, ideally, ought to be marital.

This effectively means replacing sex-ed with marriage and family education. Because to speak of the possibility of children at the time of sexual intercourse is to raise the question of the partners' future relationship. It is to speak of the possibility of parenting a common child. This is inextricably tied to a conversation regarding relationships between men and women, preparation for marriage, and the skills marriage requires. A conversation about what premarital behavior prepares for and strengthens marriage, is also more than warranted.

This recommendation seems almost too obvious, given how much of life's personal happiness, and the happiness of future generations, depends

---

[8] US Department of Health and Social Services, Replicating Evidence-Based Teen Pregnancy Prevention Programs to Scale in Communities with the Greatest Need (Grants, Tier 1B) (Fiscal Years 2015–2019).

[9] US Department of Health and Human Services, "State Abstinence Education Grant Program Fact Sheet," Family and Youth Services Bureau (April 28, 2015).

upon marriage. The vast majority of Americans marry. The vast majority parent children. In the words of Anthony Giddens, too much has been left to men and women to "decision."[10] The meanings of sex and marriage are so many and so altered, that we need to provide the information and the good will for a new contract between men and women which will be fair, and will attend to reality. I am suggesting that we approach such a new contract by first giving both parties more information about one another, about sex, about healthy relationships and marriage, and about what children need.

Young Americans are ready for this. Sex-ed as currently conducted is not highly regarded by many. Teens do not find it particularly helpful or interesting, according to a 2016 study.[11] Historian Jeffrey Moran, author of a leading account of twentieth century sex education, questions the idea that students will simply "respond rationally to information given them." He suggests instead that the "critical question is not whether students understand the mechanics of the condom but whether their vision of their own life is such that preventing pregnancy or avoiding disease is important enough for the condom to seem relevant."[12] He proposes that only education that touches on their most important relationships, and their hopes for the future, can begin to influence their incremental choices about sex and parenting.

Furthermore, the results of current sex-ed programs are less than impressive. Today, even according to supporters of such programs, very few of the federally supported evidence-based programs have positive or lasting effects on teen pregnancy rates.[13]

A large 2016 UK study of sex education – involving programs in Africa, Latin America and Europe, covering 55,000 participants, and relying only upon randomized control trials and objective measures – concluded that they did not have any measurable effect on nonmarital pregnancy rates.[14] Although

[10] Anthony Giddens, "Affluence, Poverty, and the Idea of a Post-Scarcity Society," UN Research Institute for Social Development (Discussion Paper, DP63, May 1995), www.unrisd.org/80256B3C005BCCF9/(httpAuxPages)/D04C41AAF1FA94FF80256B67005B67B8/$file/dp63.pdf.

[11] Mandy Oaklander, "Sex Ed is Negative, Sexist and Out of Touch: Study," *Time Magazine*, September 12, 2016, www.time.com/4488013/sex-education-sexism-abstinence/.

[12] Jeffrey Moran, *Teaching Sex: The shaping of adolescence in the 20th century* (Cambridge: Harvard University Press, 2000), 220.

[13] Ron Haskins and Greg Margolis *Show Me the Evidence: Obama's Fight for Rigor and Results in Social Policy* (Washington, DC: Brookings Institution Press, 2014): 67–101.

[14] Amanda J. Mason-Jones et al., "School-based interventions for preventing HIV, sexually transmitted infections, and pregnancy in adolescents," *Cochrane Database of Systematic Reviews* 11 (2016), Art. No.: CD006417, DOI: 10.1002/14651858.CD006417.pub3., www.onlinelibrary.wiley.com/doi/10.1002/14651858.CD006417.pub3/epdf/standard.

they did find that incentives to stay in school – such as cash payments or free school uniforms – reduced STI and pregnancy rates in poorer areas.

Marriage programs should include the research about marriage as a superior context for children, especially as compared to cohabitation or other nonmarital arrangements. They should also address the importance of parents' peaceful and generous mutual support for one another and for a mutual relationship with the child. They should include a discussion of the risk factors for lasting marriage, including nonmarital sex and cohabitation with any person other than the person one is engaged to marry. At the very least, they should incorporate an emphasis on sexual delay, not only because contraception fails, and earlier parenting is associated with a host of social difficulties, but also because earlier and more frequent nonmarital sex is associated with weakening male/female relationships over the long run, and diminishing marital happiness and eventually children's well-being.[15]

A realistic component of marriage education would be a description of the current markets for sex, dating and marriage, as I have described them in this text. Such education would point out how new "freedoms" and new problems go hand in hand, especially from the perspective of feminists and the poor. This can be integrated with a discussion about the two-fold reality of sex – as bonding couples and creating new life. It should highlight the difficulties of current relationship markets, especially for women and the poor.

There is no reason why marriage education could not include a component about self-discipline and willpower. These are a science on their own. They can be learned or strengthened. Experiments have yielded recommendations about habits such as pre-commitment, taking the long view, setting higher goals, practicing, gaining self-awareness, having clear goals and specific strategies, and avoiding decision fatigue.[16]

In addition, effective communication skills are increasingly understood to serve marital stability, as are practical discussions about marital sex, finances, and domestic life. Information about age at marriage might also be useful. Current findings indicate that, while very young marriage is associated with problems including divorce, delaying marriage until one's thirties is *also* correlated with higher divorce rates.[17] Delaying marriage for

---

[15] Dean M. Busby et al., "Sowing Wild Oats: Valuable Experience or a field full of weeds?" *Personal Relations* 20 (2013: 706–718); and Dean M. Busby et al., "Compatibility or restraint? The Effects of Sexual Timing on Marriage Relationships," *Journal of Family Psychology* 24 (2010): 766–774.

[16] Roy F. Baumeister and John Tierney, *Willpower: Rediscovering the Greatest Human Strength* (New York: Penguin, 2012).

[17] Jason S. Carroll, "For Love or Money? The Economic Consequences of Delayed Marriage," *The Family in America* 30 (2016) 1–17.

education may advantage many, but for perhaps as many as two-thirds of the population, it might be wiser to put marriage-mindedness on the horizon earlier.[18]

The aim of marriage education is not to idealize marriage – which would also be a problem for its stability.[19] Realism is desirable, especially in the face of repeated findings that more disadvantaged Americans may tend to over-idealize marriage and feel unworthy to enter or maintain it. I detect – if not a groundswell – at least some serious and important support for the idea of marriage education beginning long before individuals are thinking about marriage. Scholars increasingly understand that money is not the only impediment to marriage among the poorer, but also matters of trust, relationship quality, and mutual appreciation for the opposite sex.[20] One sees these needs voiced poignantly by low-income women, especially in Edin and Kefalas' *Promises I Can Keep*. Sara McLanahan has also reflected that marriage promotion could be coincident with feminist goals of building mutual understanding and couple communication, if it addresses these subjects alongside the problems of gender mistrust and sexual infidelity which are prominent in some communities.[21]

There appears to be an unmet demand for marriage education. Some colleges are filling it with courses about relationships and dating, which are reportedly oversubscribed and enthusiastically received.[22] A growing number of young adult groups, such as Grupo Solido, Corazon Puro, the Love and Fidelity Network and others, are developing curricula. Various websites and private groups are also stepping in.[23]

A second place where the federal government should link sex with child welfare is in the fact sheets it makes available to the public on its health websites or wherever sexual expression is publicly discussed. A larger and likely more important project, however, would be a large-scale public communications campaign about the advantages of marital parenting. This is one of the leading

---

[18] See Kay Hymowitz et al., *Knot Yet: The Benefits and Costs of Delayed Marriage in America* (The National Marriage Project at the University of Virginia, 2013).

[19] Stephanie Coontz, *The Way We Never Were: American Families and the Nostalgia Trap* (New York: Basic Books, 1992).

[20] Daniel Schneider, "Lessons Learned from Non-Marriage Experiments," *The Future of Children* 25 (2015): 155–78, 173.

[21] Sara McLanahan, *Diverging Destinies*, 623.

[22] See, e.g., Richard Weissbourd et al., "Preparing Students for Romantic Relationships," *Education Week*, January 10, 2014 www.edweek.org/ew/articles/2013/12/01/kappan_weissbourd .html.

[23] See, e.g., The Dibble Institute, "Resources for Teaching Relationship to Teens and Young Adults," at www.dibbleinstitute.org/.

suggestions in the Brookings/AEI joint report on poverty.[24] An existing federal partner, NCTUP, claims that it has been successful in marketing "safe sex" messages to women of twenty and older.[25] The federal government should partner with this or another group to promote a campaign on behalf of children.

Perhaps the most important place for the federal government to communicate about children's needs and interests at the front door is in its contraception programs. First and foremost because this is the moment – the moment of thinking about using contraception – which is also the moment in which the child could be made. This is an important venue for communication because contraception programs are so large and touch so many people. It is important because so many people have mistakenly come to believe that federal support for contraception constitutes sufficient attention to children. It is also the right venue because of current programs' internally contradictory message that we should care passionately about children, but not at the moment of their creation. Finally, large contraception programs will undoubtedly continue. They enjoy robust support at the federal level from both Democrats and Republicans. The best one can do is to assist them to provide a much more balanced and child-protective message.

To do this, we have to overcome the fear that it is impossible to criticize contraception or contraceptive programs. Even evidence-based critiques can easily be met with harsh public judgments, as in this reporter's response[26] to the idea that women are immiserated by contraception's separation of sex from children: "only the right-wing patriarchy would trash a technological innovation that supported an age of social and political progress for women."

It is too late for even these types of attempted conversation-stopping judgments to prevent a new approach. The contraception programs are a disappointment on their own terms. Economists and sociologists have convincingly explained how women and the poor are immiserated due in part to the way in which these programs ignore their preferences and opportunity costs.

Furthermore, there is also a growing voice of women who feel empowered to critique often powerful hormonal drugs and devices produced by large corporations and targeted exclusively to women. They may be women who

---

[24] Brookings Institution and American Enterprise Institute, *Opportunity, Responsibility and Security: A Consensus Plan for Reducing Poverty and Restoring the American Dream*, 33.

[25] The National Campaign to Prevent Teen and Unplanned Pregnancies, *Unplanned Pregnancy Among College Students and Strategies to Address It*, July 2015, www.thenationalcampaign. org/sites/default/files/resource-primary-download/briefly-_unplanned_pregnany_college.pdf); http://thenationalcampaign.org/about/what-we-do.

[26] Christina Sterbenz, "The Economics of Sex Theory Is Completely Wrong," *Business Insider*, March 3, 2014, www.businessinsider.com/economics-of-sex-video-debunked-2014-2.

are unsatisfied with contraception because of its effects on their health, or because of the demands of the new sex and marriage marketplaces it has facilitated. They regularly feel empowered to speak *because* of feminism and not to spite it.[27] They don't envision or position themselves as modern-day Lysistratas or June Cleavers. They are rather seeking to put the union between men and women on a footing that incorporates and respects women's sexual experience too, body and mind.

Were the government willing to speak about children in connection with private decisions to use contraception, what would it say? I look for analogies to several "cautions" issued by the government in the name of preserving health or promoting environmental responsibility. One analogy is the Surgeon General's health warning on a cigarette package – which also took more than a decade after it was first proposed, and a quarter century after the scientific evidence emerged.[28] A second analogy comes from proposed environmental warnings on gas-guzzling in light of climate change. For example, it has been proposed in California, and adopted in North Vancouver, Canada to attach a carbon dioxide warning to gasoline pumps reading something like this: "Gasoline consumption releases Co2, a greenhouse gas determined by the State of California to contribute to global warning. For ways to reduce gas consumption, go to: www.CityofBerkeley.gov."[29]

The government might structure its message about contraception as follows, in light of my more generalized recommendations above:

> Sex is significant not only because it makes an important connection between the adults involved, but also because it makes babies. The moment of conception is also the moment that a child's family structure is formed. Family structure matters. Parents create their children's family structure when they have sex, and a stable healthy marriage is the best place for children. If you get in the habit of distancing yourself emotionally and mentally from sexual partners and from the children you might create, it could be harder for you to form a strong marriage later, or for you and your spouse to become dedicated parents. In addition to its health effects on women, it is possible

---

[27] See, e.g., Holly Grigg-Spall, *Sweetening the Pill: or How We Got Hooked on Hormonal Birth Control* (Alresford, UK: Zero Books, 2013).

[28] Robert N. Proctor, "The history of the discovery of the cigarette-lung cancer link: evidentiary traditions, corporate denial, global toll," *Tobacco Control* 21 (2012):87–91, www.ncbi.nlm.nih.gov/pmc/articles/PMC3725195/.

[29] Tamara, Baluja, "Climate change stickers mandatory on North Vancouver pumps: Stickers to warn that burning fossil fuels causes climate change," *CBC News*, British Columbia, November 17, 2015, www.cbc.ca/news/canada/british-columbia/north-vancouver-climate-change-stickers-gas-pumps-1.3323621.

that widespread reliance on contraception increases the pressure on women to participate in sex they don't really want, and thereby also increases rates of nonmarital birth and abortion.

How would the government deliver this message? One might ask how it has delivered its current message of sexual expressionism: through everything from the research it chooses to fund, to the guidance it provides doctors indirectly and women directly, to any Food and Drug Administration policies on informed consent, to its rhetoric in judicial opinions and in its other official legal pronouncements, to its rhetoric in *amicus* briefs and while speaking at its various bully pulpits. The federal government also has to grapple with the question of the partnerships it forms. As described in Chapter One, the government needs to jettison partners promoting insufficient responsibility or even irresponsibility respecting nonmarital childbearing. Alternatively, it needs to require them to change their messages and to encourage adult responsibility at conception by incorporating the above general and specific admonitions.

It would also be wise if the government at the very least ceased struggling against those religious institutions with good track records for linking sex and children with marriage. Several of the major religions in the United States hold a view of sexual expression which would capacitate couples to be more stably united, and would help adults incorporate concern for children's into their thinking about sex. There is historical evidence that religious beliefs have favorably impacting premarital pregnancy rates in the United States.[30] Researchers also regularly observed today by researchers that practicing believers of various religious traditions enjoy better family outcomes.[31] Additionally, religious bodies are more often interweaving their teachings about sexual and family norms with respected empirical data.[32]

The state can encourage religions to help without governmental endorsement or payment for proselytization. The federally sponsored Faith Based Initiatives are practiced at drawing these lines.[33] Today, politicians and scholars across the ideological spectrum appear more willing to invite in religious and nonreligious

[30] Alan C. Carlson, "Puritans, Victorians, post-war Catholics: Images from America's sexual history: Sexuality as a litmus test of culture," *Mercatornet*, October 16, 2015, www.mercatornet. com/articles/view/puritans-victorians-post-war-catholics-images-from-americas-sexual-history/ 17020#sthash.YXD58NFf.dpuf.

[31] Edward O. Laumann and Yoosik Youm, "Sexual Expression in America," in, *Sex, Love, and Health in America: Private Choices and Public Policies*, ed. Edward O. Laumann and Robert T. Michael (Chicago: The University of Chicago Press, 2001): 109–147, 126.

[32] See, e.g., Bruce Wydick, "Why Married Sex is Social Justice," *Christianity Today*, June 23, 2016.

[33] See, e.g., 45 Code of Federal Regulations 87, 1050 (2016).

civil society to better assist children by assisting marriage. This is one of the consensus recommendations of the Brookings/AEI report on poverty alleviation.[34]

CONTINUING OBJECTIONS

Impossibility

Before I conclude, allow me to address several possible objections to my proposals, in addition to those I have already treated. First, many are convinced
that there is no way to "reinvent sex." This is not a new thought. Just before it
was "reinvented" or "transformed" in the twentieth century[35] many observers
likely held the same belief. This is the fallacy of the present – its tendency
to appear "permanent and natural."[36] The long view, however, described by
historian Yuval Harari in his book *Sapiens*, may be more accurate. He writes
that despite "[m]illions of years of evolution [which] have designed us to live
and think as community members ... [w]ithin a mere two centuries we have
become alienated individuals. Nothing testifies better to the awesome power
of culture." He concludes further that sapiens can choose to "transform social
structures and the nature of their interpersonal relations, their economic activities a host of other behaviors within a decade or two."[37] This merits trying for
all of the reasons proposed in this book.

As I have noted several times before in this volume, we should take encouragement from current political and ideological agreement about the goods of
marital parenting and about the meaning of emerging research on family structure and its relationship to child outcomes. Furthermore, it is no longer realistic
to believe that you can get to a place of healthy, stable parental unions providing
sufficient care for children, without more attention to the benefits of healthy
male/female relations, or marriage and marital childbearing. Several of the
greatest champions of "back door" or contraception programs acknowledge this.

Harvard's Robert Putnam, for example – one of the great champions of the
position that Americans need to assist *other* people's children – "doesn't dispute that we need to fix families to fix poverty."[38] He simply and rightly pairs

---

[34] Brookings Institution and American Enterprise Institute, *Opportunity, Responsibility and
      Security: A Consensus Plan for Reducing Poverty and Restoring the American Dream*, 33.
[35] Giddens, *The Transformation of Intimacy*; and Jonathan Eig, *The Birth of the Pill: How Four
      Crusaders Reinvented Sex and Launched A Revolution.*
[36] Alan Bloom, *Love and Friendship* (New York: Simon and Schuster, 1993), 29.
[37] Yuval Noah Harari, *Sapiens: A Brief History of Humankind* (New York: HarperCollins, 2015), 360, 34.
[38] Emily Badger, "The terrible loneliness of growing up poor in Robert Putnam's America," *The
      Washington Post*, March 6, 2015, www.washingtonpost.com/news/wonk/wp/2015/03/06/the-
      terrible-loneliness-of-growing-up-poor-in-robert-putnams-america/?utm_term=.515c1555d1ec.

the need for that effort with an argument about the need to boost real wages and blue-collar jobs, among other efforts. Isabel Sawhill, a strong supporter of LARCs solution, still opines that while there is a "tendency to think that marriage is something that only conservatives care about ... [l]iberals should care about it as well" for the reason that "[i]f you care about poverty, if you care about inequality and social mobility, you have to focus on and care about what's been happening to the family and to marriage in America."[39]

Other scholars agree. Professor John Witte writes that the "most important response" to nonmarital births is a "more robust legal and cultural embrace of marriage as the best institution for having and raising children."[40] Brookings scholar David Ribar deduces the same answer following his thorough review of governmental attempts to "make up" for a child's loss of married parent. He concludes that "[w]hile interventions that raise incomes, increase parental time availability, provide alternative services, or provide other in-kind resources would surely benefit children, these are likely to be, at best, only partial substitutes for marriage itself. The advantages of marriage for children appear to be the sum of many, many parts."[41]

Furthermore, we have some experience in the U.S. of getting past even difficult disputes about voluntary sexual behavior and coming together when suffering is apparent. In recent memory, this would include the fight against AIDS. For decades it commanded huge national resources, dedicated research, and public exhortation. We are in a better place because of it.

There are other indications too, that now is the time for this effort. Reports issued in 2016 indicate important reductions in nonmarital sex in younger generations as compared with older ones, and less sexual experience among high school students.[42] In a *Washington Post* interview about these reports, younger Americans spoke about everything from their higher priorities to their distaste for meaningless sex.[43] Sociologist Nicholas Wolfinger showed

[39] Nathan Pippenger, "Arguments Q + A: Isabel Sawhill, Author of Generation Unbound," *Democracy: A Journal of Ideas*, October 17, 2014, www.democracyjournal.org/arguments/arguments-qa-isabel-sawhill-author-of-generation-unbound/.

[40] John Witte, *The Sins of the Fathers: The Law and Theology of Illegitimacy Reconsidered* (Cambridge: Cambridge University Press, 2009), 182.

[41] David C Ribar, "Why Marriage Matters for Child Wellbeing," *Future of Children* 25 (Fall 2015): 11–27, 23.

[42] US Centers for Disease Control, *Trends in the prevalence of sexual behavior and HIV testing, National YTBS: 1991–2015* (2016), www.cdc.gov/healthyyouth/data/yrbs/pdf/2015/ss6506_updated.pdf.

[43] Jean Twenge et al., "Sexual inactivity during young adulthood is more common among U.S. millennials and iGen: Age, period, and cohort effects on having no sexual partners after age 18," *Archives of Sexual Behavior* (Online, 2016) doi: 10.1007/s10508-016-0798-z; Jean Twenge, et al., "Changes in American adults' sexual behavior and attitudes, 1972–2012," *Archives of Sexual Behavior* 44 (2016): 2273–2285.

that, while only five percent of women entered marriage as virgins, another twenty-two percent had sexual intercourse only with the man they married.[44] This does not compare with rates forty years ago, but neither is it nothing. It is a base to stand on.

There also remains not insubstantial discomfort with nonmarital sex and single parenting. According to Pew Research reports, large majorities of Americans disfavor both, including majorities of those in communities experiencing high rates of single parenting.[45]

We also know that parents would appreciate support as they try to channel their children's behavior toward sexual health and stable marriage. They would warmly welcome more support from the state. In the forlorn words of one female college student, interviewed for a "hookup culture" book. "The only people telling me not to do this stuff are my parents."[46]

Privacy and Stigma

Some are concerned about the government violating the private realm of relationships, or restigmatizing especially single motherhood and nonmarital children. These objections do not carry the weight they would have carried years ago – prior to the federal government's bold sexual expression advocacy, or its stepped-up involvement with family life at the back door and contraception at the front.

The government is already deeply entrenched in the conversation about sex and marriage and parenting. There are too many buses swathed in state-supported advertisements for STI testing, too many grants to Planned Parenthood and NCTUP, and too many state-subsidized marriage billboards and contraception programs to argue that it is a violation of privacy or personal sensibilities for the government to enter the domains of sex, marriage and parenting. I am requesting only that when it *does* enter, as it has and will, it takes up the cause of vulnerable children at the front door.

Regarding the fear of stigma, I have two thoughts. First, it seems unlikely, given our past century of frank talk about everything sexual, and our increased

---

44 Nicholas H. Wolfinger, "Counterintuitive Trends in the Link Between Premarital Sex and Marital Stability," Institute for Family Studies (June 6, 2016), www.family-studies.org/counter-intuitive-trends-in-the-link-between-premarital-sex-and-marital-stability/.

45 Pew Research Center, "Disapprove of Single Mothers," *Factank: News in the Numbers,* January 6, 2011, http://www.pewresearch.org/fact-tank/2011/01/06/disapprove-of-single-mothers/; Pew Research Center, "As Marriage and Parenthood Drift Apart, Public Is Concerned about Social Impact," July 1, 2007, www.pewsocialtrends.org/2007/07/01.

46 Laura Sessions Stepp, *Unhooked: How Young Women Pursue Sex, Delay Love and Lose at Both* (New York: Riverhead Books, 2007), 79.

understanding of the pressures that lead to nonmarital parenting. Second, even if it's possible, it's time to take the risk. There are stigmas associated with practically every family choice imaginable. I remember the snide comments about my "abandoning my children to be raised by others" when I chose to work after having children. Ex-spouses and step-parents know stigma too. But the individual and social costs of nonmarital childbearing are mounting beyond what we should bear. And the poor are suffering most.

My positive proposals, and invitations to do better by children, are far superior to the former method – illegitimacy laws. They are inspired by ethical principles, such as informed consent, duties to the vulnerable and to those we create, duties to the future we are building now, and duties to act on the knowledge we have. My proposals also have the potential to assist adult relationships, and to better achieve the interests of women, especially poor women.

CONCLUSION

Saturday Night Live comedian Norm MacDonald had a joke that began with a quotation from a Hollywood actress who "says that she does not mind if the man she's married to cheats on her, explaining, quote, 'Sexual experimentation is a basic need of all men'. You can read more about Goldie Hawn's personal philosophy in my new book: *Goldie Hawn: The Greatest Woman Who Ever Lived*."[47]

By this standard, I am guessing that I am the least woman who ever lived, which is something I have kept in mind throughout my writing of this book. The degree to which sexual expression – unmindful of children and of marriage – is part of everything that is considered to be "progress" today, is daunting.

But I have a different view of progress. It isn't technological wizardry, or freedom from the demands of others. It can't be inherited from a prior generation. It rather means that actors with free will, including governments, choose to be responsible for those people given into their care in their own generation, especially those most in need.

---

[47] Saturday Night Live Transcripts, Season 22: Episode 9, " Weekend Update with Norm MacDonald," snltranscripts.jt.org/96/96iupdate.phtml.

Index